# FLOWERS

## FOR THE HOME

Influences from the World Over
by Prudence Designs

GRAYSON HANDY
AND TRACEY ZABAR

PHOTOGRAPHS BY
ELLEN SILVERMAN

FOREWORD BY
PAULETTE COLE

RIZZOLI
NEW YORK

First published in the United States of America
in 2009 by Rizzoli International Publications, Inc.
300 Park Avenue South
New York, New York 10010
www.rizzoliusa.com

Photography copyright © 2009 by Ellen Silverman

2009 2010 2011 2012 / 10 9 8 7 6 5 4 3 2 1

Printed in China
ISBN 978-0-8478-3334-4
Library of Congress Control Number: 2009928420

Project Editor: Sandra Gilbert
Art Director: Ivette Montes de Oca, Overlap Design

PAGES 4: (TOP ROW, LEFT TO RIGHT) CHINESE DYNASTY:
A TEA CANISTER HAS BEEN ADORNED WITH ROSES. ENGLISH
ROSE: GOLD CROWNS ARE FILLED WITH VELVETY ROSES.
FRENCH BOUDOIR: A SILK RIBBON HAS BEEN FESTOONED
WITH A PINK PEONY PETAL AND EIFFEL TOWER, FRENCH
POODLE, AND VICTORIAN HAND CHARMS. (MIDDLE ROW,
LEFT TO RIGHT) INDIAN SARI: PHALAENOPSIS ORCHIDS
SPRINKLED ACROSS A SIMPLE TABLE APPEAR JEWEL-LIKE.
JAPANESE KIMONO: THE COLORS OF THIS DELICATE PEONY
ECHO THOSE OF THE GEISHA'S FLOWING KIMONO. MEXICAN
ALTAR: A FLORAL-PAINTED MEXICAN BOWL IS THE PERFECT
VESSEL TO FLOAT BURGUNDY DAHLIAS AND CANDLES.
(BOTTOM ROW, LEFT TO RIGHT) MOROCCAN MEDINA: THIS
GLOWING BRASS LANTERN IS SURROUNDED BY A PROFUSION
OF ORANGE DAHLIA FLOWER HEADS. SOUTHERN ROOTS:
VARIEGATED AND RED DAHLIAS ARE PERFECT FOR A SUMMER
PARTY. TROPICAL RAIN FOREST: FUCHSIA CATTLEYA OR-
CHIDS AND A SUCCULENT ECHEVERIA ADORN A COCONUT
VASE. 7: THERE IS SOMETHING TO BE SAID FOR THE PURITY
OF A PLAIN GLASS CONTAINER. I LOVE BEING ABLE TO SEE
THE ABSTRACT DISPLAY OF THE STEMS OF COLORFUL
BLOOMS AND GREENERY BELOW THE WATER LINE. 8: GODE-
TIA BLOOMS, KNOWN AS A "FAREWELL-TO-SPRING," LOOK
GREAT NESTLED TOGETHER IN A MOTTAHEDEH FOOTED
BOWL. THIS BURST OF PINKS ADDS A WELCOME SPLASH OF
COLOR IN FRONT OF A COLLECTION OF CREAMWARE ON A
DARK WOOD SIDEBOARD. 11: AN OLD-FASHIONED WATERING
CAN SPROUTS AN ARRAY OF COLORFUL SNAPDRAGONS.

SPECIAL THANKS TO THE FOLLOWING WHO SHARED CHERISHED OBJECTS
AND TEXTILES FROM AROUND THE WORLD WITH ME FOR *FLOWERS FOR
THE HOME* PHOTOGRAPHY:

Calvin Klein Home (for Japanese Kimono: white and black plates; for Tropical
Rain Forest: lavender glass bowl, place settings, Hampshire stemware), Clodagh
(for Mexican Altar: carved bull head; for Tropical Rain Forest: metal basins), Ellen
Christine (for French Boudoir: lace tissue box, Venetian mirror, hat boxes; for
Southern Roots: doll-head vase); Aaron Freidus (for Japanese Kimono: silk-
covered books, print; for Chinese Dynasty: hand scroll), Deborah Gardner (for
English Rose: Staffordshire dogs), Mara Gardner (for English Rose: royal family
collectibles; for Moroccan Medina: pierced lantern), Gia Grosso (for Chinese
Dynasty: painted bottle), Kate Hirson (for Mexican Altar: bench, mercury hurricane
lanterns, silver vase, votives, painted ceramic bowls, dinnerware, ex-votos), Tom
Judd (for Chinese Dynasty: *Pink Rose* painting), Jessica Napp (for French Boudoir:
Seine photograph), Susan Lipper (for English Rose: William Morris tea towel, bis-
cuit tin, scenic postcards), Ivette Montes de Oca and Michael Zweck-Bronner (for
Japanese Kimono: teapot, bowl; for Mexican Altar: Saarinen chair; for Tropical
Rain Forest: Russel Wright china), Thomas O'Laughlin (for Tropical Rain Forest:
wooden pedestal, metal sculpture), Luis Quintero (for Mexican Altar: Fiestaware),
Justin Reyes (for Chinese Dynasty: calligraphy boxes), Ben Sander (for Southern
Roots: wicker picnic basket, red-and-white tablecloth and napkins), Lynn Scrabis
(for French Boudoir: decoupage tins), Stark Fabric (for Southern Roots: silk taffeta;
for Tropical Rain Forest: botanical printed fabric and wallpaper), Anita Trehan (for
Indian Sari: silver bowls and spoons, teas, lotus pedestal dish and bowl, dupioni
silk and other embroidered cloths), Maki Yamamoto of Fabricteria Maki (for Japan-
ese Kimono: kimonos, obi, small bench, sandals), David Zabar and Sons and
Rebecca Rose Zabar (for French Boudoir: poodle charm), and Tracey Zabar (for
French Boudoir: Eiffel Tower and Victorian hand charms).

To the best of my ability, I have been factual, and I hope that all people involved in the
creation of this book have been credited. Needless to say, any errors or omissions are my
own and are deeply regretted.

## Dedication

*FLOWERS FOR THE
HOME* IS DEDICATED
TO ARTURO QUINTERO,
WHOSE TALENT,
STRENGTH, AND LOVE
OF FLOWERS INSPIRES
ME DAILY, AND TO
THE MEMORY OF MY
BELOVED PRUDENCE.
ALSO TO GABBY, LUPE,
AND ROMEO, WHO END
EACH HECTIC DAY
WITH *MUCHOS BESITOS.*

CHINESE DYNASTY

ENGLISH ROSE

FRENCH BOUDOIR

INDIAN SARI

JAPANESE KIMONO

MEXICAN ALTAR

MOROCCAN MEDINA

SOUTHERN ROOTS

TROPICAL RAIN FOREST

Contents

# Foreword

## BY PAULETTE COLE

you
home is your mirror
reflect your vision
the earth is our collective home
look within

FLOWERS ARE OUR miraculous tools from the heavens, entities of light and magic that we can feel and touch in this dimension. Flowers channel the essence of the fairy realm into our world, offering themselves as the ultimate design in creation, grace, and fancy. We see the universe alive in each flower, the celestial emerging through the earth and evoked by the light of the sun. In our urban environments, we thirst for connection with the earth; we are hungry to feel the order of nature in our daily lives. Flowers are the living tool we use to breathe life into the home; they are a metaphor for organic beauty in natural form. By bringing in fresh flowers, we bring in the earth, and nurture life at home. We move beyond the material to the living form, creating balance. A daily practice at ABC Home is to see home as our mirror. The space we create around us reflects our personal vision, and when our vision is realized, it mirrors back a sense of wholeness and refuge. Flowers channel beauty and power into our lives and invite us to find, reflected, our own form of self-expression. As we move through life, different flowers speak to our beings. We search for and identify flowers and house them in ourselves.

Grayson's gift is to layer worlds of beauty and color through the purity and presence of flowers. His arrangements honor the essence of faraway lands, tapping into the whole of what is manifest around the world today, and bringing that energy home. We align with Grayson in our commitment to continuing the legacy of indigenous design, an endangered species as a reflection of globalization and big business. Manifesting this design aesthetic in the world, we act to balance homogenization. Our inspiration is to move beyond the eclectic, of layering and collage, and into an integrative design of modern, timeless, cultural, and spiritual elements. As members of a global community, our individual journeys are in constant relationship with one another. As Americans, we have traveled here for generations, creating new incarnations of "home" as a melting pot, and bringing the design DNA of vast and diverse cultures. In this coexistent new world, we understand the unique relevance of integration.

At ABC, we are deeply inspired by the ways in which our global community has translated flowers—these works of art that we have been given. From the simplicity, Zen, and balance of the Japanese garden to the tenderness of the English meadow, we recognize the beauty and power of fusion in bringing these worlds together. We consider what happens when diverse life forms enter a room; we strive to balance the feminine and the masculine, creating a sense of order and also of energy. We feel reverence for garlands in India—sacred life strung together, the concept of flowers as offerings. We love marigolds and roses, woven together or strewn as petals. We are drawn to the lotus because it is the only flower that seeds itself, a reminder that we must nurture ourselves from within. We align with the graceful, magical, feminine spirit found in wildflowers, dandelions, verbena, cornflowers, thistle, pincushion flowers, jasmine greens. Arranging the meadow inside the home in an organic way is grounding. Tree moss, cactus, and lichen bring in succulence. We honor foliage in all its different forms, as sculptural, and not just as colorful.

In a time when so much attention and appreciation is being dedicated to a cultural shift toward green consciousness, it seems all the more meaningful that we take the opportunity to learn and grow with other species around us. It is a beautiful moment for this book to be released, deepening our understanding of and relationship to flowers, one of the greatest gifts on this planet.

# Flowers

## for the Home

I love books. For me, going into a bookstore is like granting a kid unsupervised access to FAO Schwarz. I race around from section to section as though I have just had too much chocolate or coffee. Travel, fashion, art, photography, and Eastern philosophy are the aisles that stop me dead in my tracks. Here I find a treasure trove of ideas for my "global" arrangements. Several destinations and cultures have left their imprint on me. Let's be clear—not everyone has the resources, time, or freedom to jet around. No worries, though; you can always be an "armchair traveler" with books and the Internet close at hand. My first trip abroad was to London, largely because there was no language barrier and I had a dear friend, Yasmine, on the other side of the "pond" to meet me. I became fascinated by Great Britain's rich heritage, in particular the landmarks made of "old stones" (a term my European friends jokingly use to underscore the newness of America). London not only wetted my appetite to continue to travel, but also to venture to more exotic places. The next trip was certainly that. I landed in the Moroccan city of Casablanca.

From the moment I descended from the plane, I felt transported to another world. After a few nights, I made my way to Marrakech. It was all I had imagined and more. One evening my travel companion, Philippe, and I ventured into the medina for dinner. I thought it odd that the restaurant asked for each guest's name when placing the reservation. Once seated, it all made sense. Our names had been spelled out in rose petals and blue sequins at our place settings. So simple, yet so thoughtful. This lovely gesture had an

impact on me. Later, when asked by a dear friend to help him plan his marriage proposal, I knew exactly what to do to ensure an astounding *yes*. After the couple left their hotel for dinner, I snuck into their room with boxes of red rose petals and candles in tow. On the crisp white sheets, I spelled out *Marry me?* in petals. Upon their return to the candlelit suite, he dropped to one knee and presented the ring. Of course the answer was yes.

As I travel both here and abroad, it becomes more apparent that people are basically the same—we share more similarities than differences. There is a universal appreciation of beauty. For *Flowers for the Home*, I have selected nine locales that have sparked my imagination—China, England, France, India, Japan, Mexico, Morocco, the Tropical Rain Forest, and my childhood home, the American South. When I examine these areas of the world, each has a unique sensibility that is influenced by cultural traditions—from the flavors of the local cuisine and the colors and textures of the fabrics to the distinctive home furnishings. My floral arrangements reflect my personal impressions of each locale. I am always eager for the next adventure.

Get into the creative spirit with my simple floral compositions, evocative of far-flung places that are so dear to me. They demonstrate the basic principles of successful floral design—form, scale, color, texture, balance, and function. Throughout you will also find practical tips on decorating and entertaining surrounded by flowers at home. Realizing that not everyone has the luxury of being in New York City with many resources only a subway stop away, the selection of flowers has been tailored to those that are widely available. I hope that I will inspire the florist within you to be creatively fearless.

# Chinese Dynasty

WITH SUCH COLOSSAL MONUMENTS AS THE FORBIDDEN CITY AND THE

GREAT WALL, CHINA HAS A RICH HERITAGE IN WHICH FLOWERS PLAY A SYMBOLIC

ROLE. TO CAPTURE THE FLAVOR OF THIS ANCIENT CIVILIZATION, CREATE AN

INSTANT ALTAR—A DEVOTIONAL OFFERING OF LOTUS PODS AND GLORIOSA LILIES

PLACED AROUND A BUDDHA HEAD FOR AN AURA OF SOOTHING MEDITATION.

ADD A BACKDROP OF GOLDEN GINKGO LEAVES.

# The Inspirations

China's love of flowers is pervasive. There are multiple favorites: orchids, chrysanthemums, lotus, azaleas, and cherry blossoms. These blooms, along with butterflies, dragonflies, and exotic birds, embellish everything—from lacquerware, enamels, and paper lanterns to parasols, silks, and fans. Garden pavilions and pagodas with carved flora and fauna designs are omnipresent in this landscape. Elaborate ceremonial robes and other textiles are embroidered with floral patterns.

This country's festivals, with their processions of breathtaking blooms, are extraordinary. The very best time to witness one is during Chinese New Year, with its riotous multicolored roses, chrysanthemums, sunflowers, and "lucky" bamboo. Families spend the last day of the year at flower markets and fairs purchasing appropriate blooms, such as camellias, peach blossoms, and the peony, which is believed to bring good luck in the coming year. Other plants that are part of the festivities include the tangerine and pomelo, and camphor leaves, whose aroma is thought to banish bad luck. Flowers and plants have traditional blessings associated with them—wishing a long life, happiness, and prosperity to every generation. The lotus symbolizes purity and enlightenment and is unique for its ability to blossom and bear fruit at the same time. It is, for me, the quintessential expression of China. For a Chinese-themed party, tuck a few pastel-colored blossoms into a fanciful display of delicate fans.

BEYOND CHINA'S SYMBOLIC flowers, there are other icons associated with the notion of a lucky life. Since they reproduce in abundance, carp are symbols of fertility. The imperial dragon is a mystical creature that brings rain and a plentiful harvest. But more important than these symbols is the concept of yin and yang, where opposites are harmoniously intertwined. This idea plays a pivotal role in Chinese tradition. Here, an arrangement of 'Léonidas' roses and whorls of pieris make a composition of dark and light that illustrates this striving for balance.

Another enduring practice is the art of calligraphy. To create the distinctive characters of this script, ink is applied with special brushes on parchment. The hand scroll, an ancient form of bookbinding, is secured with a silk cord. Historically, scrolls were adorned with scenes depicting the seasons, as well as idyllic retreats amid mountainous landscapes of lush bamboo, fantastic rocks, and sculpted pines. Temples built in Buddha's honor cover the terrain. Viewing such epic scenes can take you on an imaginary, yet intimate, journey.

(RIGHT AND BOTTOM) Scrolls containing calligraphy and depictions of serene landscapes often have brocade mountings covered with floral patterns. Pretty boxes covered in silk contain calligraphy accoutrements—ink, brushes, brush pots, and soapstone seals. Even the surfaces of snuff bottles are decorated with such imagery.

(ABOVE, LEFT) My favorite deity is Kuan-Yin, goddess of compassion. At home, she sits in a place of honor on a lacquer stand in front of a Chinese-red cabinet. She holds one hot-pink stem of a gloriosa lily.

(RIGHT) I am always on the lookout for unusual containers for my arrangements. The variety of porcelain vessels created during the dynastic periods—from elegant Sung blue-white ware to highly decorated Ming vases—is tantalizing. For a Chinese celebration, I have used a tea canister with an image of a beautiful woman. A study of roses of various hues creates a strong statement, especially with a feminine parasol backdrop. Another way to achieve visual impact is to use one type of monochromatic flower.

# The Colors

The color palette of China is as varied as its many provinces. Although red is most often associated with this country, tones of golden yellow, pastel pink, bright purple, inky black, and jade green are equally prominent. Deep blue paired with pure white or celadon green is a popular combination found on traditional Chinese porcelain. These colors contrast nicely with such oft-used materials as rice paper, teak, and bamboo. Accents of gold embellish everything—from lacquer boxes to statuary. Vibrant silks are favored for traditional clothing. The cheongsam, a woman's tight-fitting dress with frog fasteners, is a stellar example. These adorable and colorful waving kitties, usually associated with Japan, are also beloved in China. They are thought to bring good luck, visitors, and something flowers always need more of—rain.

19

*I* ADORE CHINESE CUISINE, especially since it offers something delectable for everyone—even vegetarians like me. An old Chinese proverb says, "When you have only two pennies left in the world, buy a loaf of bread with one, and a lily with the other." This philosophy can be wonderfully expressed in your interpretation of a traditional Chinese banquet. Add garnishes of radishes and other vegetables carved in the shape of roses to the display of dishes and beautiful flowers. For casual sit-down, family-style dinners or festive banquets, use a long, red-lacquer tea table with comfortable floor cushions or ceramic garden stools as seating. Start the party with dim sum—steamed pork, chicken, and vegetable dumplings and bok choy rolls—served in bamboo steamers lined with banana leaves. Add a blossom or two as a fanciful accent. Brightly colored bowls for noodles, rice, and dipping sauces, accompanied with chopsticks, make a striking tabletop for a main course of stir-fried chicken with greens. Finish the look with red floral linens and matching flowers. An alternative color scheme is Chinese blue and white. If you are a disaster in the kitchen, call on your local Chinese restaurant and have the food delivered. Many hosts prefer to transfer the take-out dinner into their own serving dishes. Traditional white rice bowls of varying sizes look great near a simple arrangement of tightly packed orange chrysanthemums in a white cylindrical vase. End the meal with a plate of fortune cookies containing whimsical sayings and florid prose. Good-luck coin pendants, wrapped in tissue paper and tucked into silk pouches, make Chinese-style party favors.

(LEFT) Using Chinese-food take-out containers as vases is a playful way to create centerpieces. They are readily available and inexpensive. Though most restaurants use the standard white ones, some paper and specialty stores stock them in various colors, patterns, and sizes. To create a lively arrangement, fill a plastic-lined container with chartreuse chrysanthemums, 'Jade' roses, and ranunculus, and accent with hypericum berries. For a whimsical touch, top with a set of lacquered chopsticks (see page 182 for complete instructions).

21

I seldom use basic un-adorned glass vases for arrangements, but wrapping several in Chinese take-out menus or fresh leaves looks striking. Secure the covers in place with a raffia tie. Mix the vessels with simple dishes in a palette of stark white, black, or chocolate brown to create a graphic look. Bright red anemones with black centers complement the menus for a Pop art effect.

Celadon green is a divine alternative to the traditional white ground usually found in Chinese porcelain. Pink roses mixed with cymbidium orchids contrast nicely against the green. Rather than a large center-piece in the middle of the table, put a tiny, exquisite bouquet at each place setting. Diminutive Ming-style vases with a few roses each are a perfect way to add color. These twig pots and tree-trunk furniture are a great look for a Chinese-style tea party.

CHINESE-INSPIRED INTERIORS are lavish and opulent, or minimal and spiritual. Scholar's cabinets and wedding chests are often richly carved out of dark wood. Other furniture is made of dramatic, high-gloss black or red lacquer. Collections of blue-and-white porcelain are displayed in formal settings. Folding screens depict mystical landscapes full of exotic flora and fauna. Textiles, often silks or satins in saturated gem colors, are embroidered with detailed patterns. Graceful bamboo shoots, dragons, and cranes in flight are popular motifs.

Proponents of the Chinese philosophy of feng shui believe that furniture and accessories should be positioned in a room to harmonize with nature—creating a positive energy flow, or *ch'i*. When decorating, editing is essential to avoid a heavy look. The lack of clutter allows goodness, love, health, and prosperity to enter the space. One way to lighten up a room is to use plenty of white with dark colors as accents. The Chinese also have respect for the five elements of wood, water, earth, fire, and metal; there should be a balance of these in every home. Flowers, herbs, and grass are not only pleasing additions to interiors, but they also have healing qualities on the human psyche.

Hydrangeas have an amazing lacy look, especially when bunched in huge bouquets. These flowers come in many colors, from white and celadon to pink and blue—soft hues that are very calming. This versatile bloom looks great in many environments, from the formal to the casual. Here, an arrangement of white, lavender, blue, and celadon hydrangeas in a chinoiserie vase is placed atop a blue-and-white tray. The setting —a clean, white loft— allows the flowers to be the center of attention.

This gold-lacquered vase, filled with an arrangement of yellow and peach roses, ranunculus, and cymbidium orchids, can add sophistication and drama to any room. Sitting on a faux-bamboo serving cart, this simple bouquet of flowers becomes the focus of the room. A few blossoms on this *craquelure* garden stool, in a perfect shade of jade green, are a sweet touch.

# English
## Rose

ENGLAND IS THE HOME OF POMP AND PAGEANTRY, TRADITION AND
ECCENTRICITY. THE BRITS' OBSESSION WITH THE MONARCHY IS EVER PRESENT.
LIKENESSES OF THE ROYALS DOMINATE THE TABLOIDS AND APPEAR ON
ALL MANNER OF COLLECTIBLES, FROM PORCELAIN TO BISCUIT TINS. SUITABLY,
THE TUDOR ROSE IS THE NATIONAL EMBLEM. HERE, 'BLACK BEAUTY' ROSES,
COMBINED WITH CALLA LILIES, ARE AS REGAL AS THE QUEEN'S ROBE.

# The Inspirations

London, with its ubiquitous black cabs, resplendent Westminster Abbey, and the majestic Houses of Parliament, is a vibrant cultural center. The red double-decker buses, Big Ben, and the London Eye Ferris wheel are renowned icons. The city's streets bustle with men attired in Savile Row bespoke suits, nannies pushing prams, fashionable ladies with smart hats, and punks sporting Mohawks and piercings. While there, I love to roam the parks and streets and take in the flowers. The dazzling lights of Piccadilly Circus, the ceremonial Changing of the Guard at Buckingham Palace, and the grand sculpture hall at the Victoria and Albert Museum are dear to me. Weekends are spent poking about Portobello Road, where quaint Victorian storefronts are hidden by market stalls selling everything from vintage clothing to curiosities. This neighborhood is the perfect haunt to find those rare and unusual vessels for magnificent blooms.

The English countryside is dotted with sleepy, thatched-roofed hamlets, medieval castles, university towns, and crumbling estates. The village of Barlaston in Staffordshire is the home of Wedgwood, my favorite pottery and bone china manufacturer. Wedgwood's unglazed jasperware pieces depict classical Greek figures draped in tunics. The cameo relief scenes are traditionally blue and white, though they also come in many muted colors. This beige-and-white pitcher showcases creamy, pale-pink 'Sahara' roses.

WHEN HER MAJESTY Queen Elizabeth II took the throne in 1953, her coronation gown was embroidered with flora representing the United Kingdom: the English Tudor rose, the Welsh leek, the Scottish thistle, the Irish shamrock, the Canadian maple leaf, the Australian mimosa, the New Zealand fern, the South African protea, and the Indian lotus blossom. This fondness for flowers is part of the British spirit. It is customary for royals to be presented with bouquets and nosegays during visits and walkabouts.

Dating back to medieval times, nosegays regained popularity in Victorian England. The name comes from the literal meaning of these words: to make the nose gay. This fragrant fashion accessory, also called a posy or tussie-mussie, was given as a symbolic token of appreciation. Victorians communicated passion, love, and affection through a secret language of flowers, which had private meanings. This lace-bordered nosegay of velvety 'Black Beauty' roses rests atop British avantgarde fashion designer Vivienne Westwood's china. She has cleverly incorporated the design of the monarch's orb on these delightful plates.

(BOTTOM) A white peony is nestled into a Vivienne Westwood "saddle bag." Made of tartan plaid and leather, it evokes British hunting garb. I love carrying oversize bags like this one for quick trips to the flower market since they can easily hold bundles of blooms.

(ABOVE) White Staffordshire ceramic dog bookends depicting beloved pups are highly collectible. (TOP, RIGHT) Almost any vessel can be used to display flowers. I filled these gold crowns with velvety 'Hocus Pocus' roses, which complement the tones of this luxurious tartan plaid. A piece of green floral foam has been trimmed to fit this regal "vase." Once wetted, the foam holds the tightly packed arrangement in place.

(RIGHT) Tight clusters of these pastel-pink and purple hydrangeas make a bold statement without the need for additional flowers. Use an interesting vessel, such as this mirrored Hepplewhite-style cachepot. Be sure to smash the stems with a hammer before arranging the hydrangeas. This allows the blossoms to drink up more water. Since these finicky flowers tend to wilt easily, lay wet paper towels over the blossom heads; they will perk right up.

36

# The Colors

The British take their colors seriously, bestowing them with wonderfully humorous names. Reds are called scarlet, horseflesh, and maide's blush. Yellows are tawney, canary, and primrose. There are plunket, celestial, and Wedgwood blues. Greens come in popinjay, willow, even gooseturd. And neutrals aren't ignored, given names such as motley, chimney-sweep, and the amusing puke. Brits are particularly fond of pastels. These colors are beautifully displayed in the hats worn at special occasions, including Ladies' Day at Royal Ascot. Sometimes they compete for attention with the guest of honor— bride or horse. Dainty or outrageous, hats are embellished with silk or real flowers, ribbons, and feathers. Squint your eyes and you will think you are in a lovely English country garden with its palette of painterly pastels and a delightful abundance of greens.

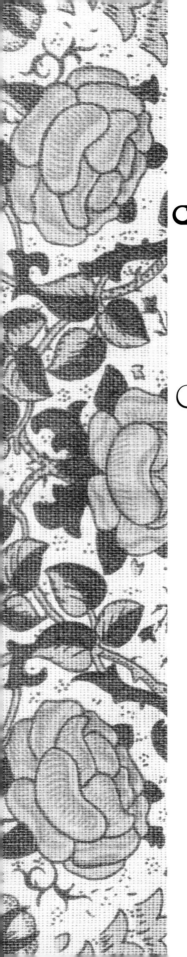

FISH AND CHIPS, pasties, bangers and mash, Yorkshire pudding, steak-and-kidney and shepherd's pies—the list of homey pub food goes on and on when one thinks of England. And, of course, there is fancier fare, including Welsh rarebit, beef Wellington, and Sunday roast. But the quintessential repast is the beloved tradition of teatime. There is a lot of ceremony attached to this sociable gathering. Tiny sandwiches of salmon, watercress, cucumber, or egg mayonnaise are served on fancy china and tiered silver trays. For a ladies' tea, desserts (called pudding) are tarts, miniature cakes, and sweet scones with clotted cream and fruity jam. The Brits usually take their afternoon tea in a sitting room in front of the fire or, when the weather permits, in the garden. As the sweet, milky tea is served on occasional or coffee tables, I like to create simple flower arrangements that take up little space. Drawing inspiration from the garden, the English pottery company Grimwades Ltd. produced ever-so-ladylike transferware in charming patterns named Sweet Pea, Anemone, Victorian Rose, Delphinium, and Floral Feast. Vintage mixed-and-matched teacups can be filled with feminine flowers (see page 182 for instructions). Pink tea roses are the perfect choice for such gatherings. A buffet for a special occasion is an excuse to create a large arrangement of assorted flowers from the cutting garden, mingled with trailing ivy, in a commanding glass vase. Set it on the center of a long table covered with a lace or linen cloth and use your best crystal and gleaming silver—candelabra, trays, and flatware. Start the cocktail hour early with Pimm's, champagne, and gin.

(LEFT) William Morris's patterned tea towels, decorated with floral motifs, are as popular today as when they were introduced during the English Arts and Crafts movement. Interlocking flowers, delicate leaves, and winding vines create complex patterns. For the flower lover, these beautifully printed textiles, as well as Morris wallpapers and tiles, are a great way of injecting even more flora into your home.

My philosophy for floral arrangements is to let the beauty of each flower shine without manipulation. Dramatic and romantic fuchsia garden roses and peonies, simply arranged in a plain glass vase, appear as if they were just plucked from the garden. Do be aware that many blooms can be quite aromatic; you don't want their overpowering scent to compete with the food.

Purple lilac, viburnum, and phlox, mixed with lavender roses, create a smashing center-piece for this garden-party setting. A simple container has been wrapped with moss matting. It is secured with twiglike wiring—a wonderful, organic touch. White and beige scalloped dinnerware contrasts nicely with the distressed garden furniture. This fresh arrangement adds a fantastic burst of color.

PLANTS AND FLOWERS can enhance any room, whether you live in a fashionable flat in town or a stately country manor. As the season changes, urns, spheres, and topiaries easily make the transition from outdoors to indoors. These ornaments age beautifully in the elements and look smart as part of the decor. Place an ivy-filled garden pot on a mantelpiece or in a niche, and surround it with a ring of sphagnum moss. Rest a clay sphere covered with moss on top.

The English home exudes comfort. The dark wood of Regency, Victorian, and Queen Anne furniture acts as a foil for floral arrangements. Velvets and rich plaids create a cozy feeling. During the Christmas holidays, these fabrics are especially stylish when accented with pine cuttings and berries. Liberty textiles, with their cheerful flower patterns, are another favorite. Portraits of beloved dogs grace the walls of English interiors. This painting of a black dachshund in a ruff by Sandro Nardini hangs against vintage botanical wallpaper, which provides the spirit of a country gentleman's library. Here, a white phalaenopsis orchid in a terra-cotta pot sits atop a faux-library-book side table. These beautiful plants, which can be expensive, do change the mood of any space.

(FOLLOWING PAGE) Ivy topiaries and climbing jasmine plants filling metal lattice garden urns, and framed pressed botanicals, are delightful touches that extend the floral theme. I am particularly fond of the botanicals' thoughtful handwritten inscriptions. Rather than hanging the prints on the wall, prop them against furniture like this garden bench. All these weathered elements create the quintessential "shabby chic" look.

# French
## Boudoir

WITHIN THE WINDING STREETS OF PARIS, EACH ARRONDISSEMENT REVEALS

ENTICING SURPRISES. *PÂTISSERIE-BOULANGERIES* DISPLAY TANTALIZING CONFECTIONS—

SOME ARE EVEN DECORATED WITH CRYSTALLIZED VIOLETS. MILLINERS PRESENT

CHIC HATS IN EXQUISITE BOXES. DID SOMEONE MENTION *L'AMOUR?* EVERYONE IS IN LOVE.

ROMANTIC COUPLES EMBRACE ON THE BANKS OF THE SEINE. WITH THEIR SENSE

OF JOIE DE VIVRE, THE FRENCH CELEBRATE BEAUTY AND PASSION IN EVERYTHING.

# The Inspirations

France's artistic, decorative, and architectural masterpieces, haute couture, and gastronomy are revered throughout the world. Such monuments as the majestic palaces of Versailles and the Louvre, the Eiffel Tower, and the Loire Valley's châteaux display virtuoso design. With their renowned attention to detail, the French are experts in creating flawless beauty. Luxurious fashions by the esteemed houses of Dior, Chanel, and Givenchy are coveted for their exquisite details. Their pricey outfits for stylish ladies are inspirations for prêt-à-porter, or ready-to-wear.

Interspersed throughout the thriving capital are delightful ornamental parks and gardens. Two of my favorites are the Tuileries and the Jardin du Luxembourg, which began as private royal pleasure gardens full of flowers and fruit trees. Laid out on a symmetrical plan, these formal French gardens include such splendid elements as reflecting pools, playful topiaries, and tree-lined paths that are balanced along a central access. Clipped parterres and hedging add structure. One of the many artists who documented the extraordinary gardens and their flowers was the Belgian Pierre-Joseph Redouté, at one time the official court artist for Marie Antoinette. He survived the Revolution, and the country's passion for roses lives on in his paintings and prints. The countryside is also breathtakingly stunning; the Provençal lavender and sunflower fields and the carefully tended vineyards of Burgundy and Bordeaux are stellar examples.

FRANCE IS SYNONYMOUS with sophisticated style and meticulous craftsmanship of the highest order. Visionary monarch Louis XIV's creation of Versailles exemplifies this striving for magnificence. A design tour de force, with its glittering Hall of Mirrors, fresco-covered ceilings, lustrous parquet floors, and palatial gardens, this palace is awe-inspiring. Even humble objects shine when coexisting with this opulent display.

For France's May Day holiday, which both honors workers and ushers in joyous springtime, vendors on every corner offer *muguets des bois,* lilies of the valley. Simple bouquets with delicate white blossoms are artfully composed. Men wear a pip (a symbol of good luck) in their buttonholes. When a lady is presented with these *fleurs,* she traditionally returns this gesture with a kiss. Don't be fooled by these tiny flowers; their fragrance can perfume an entire room. Madame's boudoir is resplendent with feminine touches like scented candles, sachets, and flowers. This sterling "Palm" vase by Christofle, filled with aromatic lilies of the valley, adds an aura of loveliness to such a private retreat.

(TOP) Rest a delicate sprig of any flower on a surface to add a touch of intrigue. Here, lily of the valley is perched on a matchbox befittingly decorated with an image of the Eiffel Tower. (BOTTOM) An embroidered lace tissue box displays a delphinium stalk.

(ABOVE) This Christofle "Libellule" vase in the Art Nouveau style is filled with purple veronica. Dragonflies, a favorite motif associated with this period, decorate this sterling-silver piece. To create a sexy French ambience, place it on a vanity in front of an opulent Venetian mirror encrusted with glass rosettes. The vase will cast a romantic reflection.

53

(RIGHT) Decoupage and toile-patterned tins make lovely decorative planters for mounds of baby's tears. The pastel hues contrast wonderfully with the vibrant green.
(OPPOSITE) *Macarons* come in flowery shades of lilac, buttercup yellow, blush pink, pistachio green, as well as coffee. These tasty sweets were made famous by the Parisian pastry shops of Ladurée and Dalloyau.

# The Colors

France is a rich tapestry of color. The outdoor markets' vegetable and flower stands, with arrays of luscious tones, are a delight to the eye. Artists have long been attracted to certain regions—in particular, Brittany and Provence—because of their inspired palettes. Brittany's picturesque coastal fishing villages are a study in blue and white. This crisp and clean color scheme dominates and examples abound—dories, sailboats, and crews clad in classic striped tops. Sun-drenched Provence is a visual bouquet of saturated colors. It is an extravaganza of tomato red, sunflower yellow, herb garden greens, and deep lavender, offset by the earthiness of the villages' ochre bricks and roof tiles. And, of course, there are Parisian flowers in soft painterly pastels of mauve, peach, and rose—hues associated with the Impressionists.

THE FRENCH ARE serious and passionate about everything gastronomical. Great care is taken in the planning of each meal; shopping every day for fresh ingredients is a requirement. A picnic would not be complete without crusty baguettes, a bottle of wine, and farmhouse cheeses. When it comes to French table settings, the approach is to achieve a gorgeous look without being too studied. A round table sets the right mood since it allows for friendly conversation. Use a low centerpiece so that guests can easily engage in spirited debate. For a special occasion, dress the table up with your prettiest porcelain, crystal flutes, and accessories. To create an informal look, use unmatched crockery. Employ the traditional Provençal color scheme of yellow, blue, and green. An empty wine bottle is a perfect vessel to hold a single bloom. Fill several with graceful French tulips. Or, compose a fuss-free display of loosely arranged, fresh-cut flowers and herbs in a rustic container. Set it on a farm table in front of an inviting hearth, and strew wild berries and fruits around. Like the French, decorate your meals with flowers. A mâche can be garnished with garden edibles, such as chive blossoms or nasturtium petals. Desserts can be fancied up with rose petals or candied violets.

For those of us who reside in a pied-à-terre with little space, the French style of entertaining can still be achieved. A painted metal bistro table with matching folding chairs can easily fit into a small kitchen or outdoor terrace. Instead of taking up precious table space with arrangements, spread the floral beauty around by filling window boxes with marguerites and herbs. And clay pots of flowers can be nestled into confined areas.

(LEFT) Fashion icon Christian Lacroix's "Continents" plates are decorated with figures of fantasy. Use colorful napkins as a framing device by placing them under these whimsical plates. This cloth, printed with the lily-shaped fleurs-de-lis, is a simple touch that continues the French mood. Clear bottle-shaped vases are filled with stems of ranunculus, peonies, grape hyacinths, and sweet pea. Sprigs of fresh mint add greenery. In keeping with the French theme, I chose whimsical Eiffel Tower place-card holders.

57

HE FRENCH HAVE perfected *the art de vivre*. Living well is an integral part of their heritage. With a legendary sense of style and elegance, they are known for chic house design. Formal interiors are a mélange of heirloom antiques and flea-market finds. Silk-brocade-covered Louis XVI armchairs and crystal chandeliers are contrasted with cheetah-patterned carpets and kitschy poodle lamps. The look is very amusing. Salons with cozy, deep sofas in front of a blazing fire and beautifully laid tables bring warmth and comfort. Toile de Jouy bed hangings with bucolic scenes of couples frolicking in the garden add an air of intimacy. Pretty flowers are everywhere—in vases, cut-crystal decanters, and perfume bottles.

Quaint country houses, some with ivy-covered facades, are usually done up in a more relaxed manner. Stone fireplaces and floors, wood ceiling beams, and faded lime-washed walls provide a neutral backdrop for colorful home furnishings, such as a painted armoire or a wrought-iron bed covered with a red-and-white-checked coverlet. To replicate this charming atmosphere, fill your home with potted flowering plants set in willow baskets and faience urns topped with balls of moss. Hang pink rose and smilax garlands over a mantelpiece to provide enchantment.

The rooftops of many French buildings are clad in copper, which acquires a green patina over time. For a rustic, French country-inspired arrangement, use a weathered tin that echoes this beautiful finish. Select varieties of peonies, roses, and begonia plants in shades of cream and white. The verdigris color of the vessel is in striking contrast to the pristine, white flowers.

(OPPOSITE) Lilac branches are loosely placed in distressed sap buckets. This rustic, Adirondack-style table, constructed of tree trunks and twigs, is the perfect pedestal to show off this casual, French-inspired display.

(LEFT) A painted wooden "fleur" box, reminiscent of those from the French flower markets, is a delightful alternative to a traditional vase. Make a tight, compact arrangement of fuchsia peonies, pastel-pink ranunculus, anemones, and grape hyacinth. Add stems of sweet pea, fresh lavender, and mint. Cascading jasmine vines soften the mix (see page 183 for complete instructions).

(OPPOSITE) While waiting for the bride to appear, Romeo, my dachshund, looks like a little prince posed on a tattered silk velvet canopy chair. A 'Sahara' rose is tucked into his bow. The French love and pamper their pooches—they join in family activities. This adorable dog deserves a treat.
(RIGHT) A sweet bridal bouquet of 'Sahara' roses is laid upon a worn, burlap-upholstered French settee. A decorative pillow with silk flower petals is the perfect feminine accent for this fairy-tale-like interior.

# Indian Sari

INDIA HOLDS A SPECIAL PLACE IN MY HEART. I LOVE THIS LAND WHERE
GODS HAVE NAMES LIKE KRISHNA, SHIVA, AND GANESHA (MY PERSONAL FAVORITE).
THE VIBRANT COLORS OF THE ELABORATE TEXTILES, GARLANDS OF MARIGOLDS
ADORNING THE PARADING ELEPHANTS, BUSTLING GEM PALACES, AND INTRICATE
MARBLE TRACERIES OF THE TAJ MAHAL ARE NOVEL. THIS CENTURIES-OLD
LAND IS A RICHLY EMBROIDERED TAPESTRY.

# The Inspirations

An abundance of flowers in a chorus of colors and pungent spices make India a paradise of the senses. There are constant reminders of the beauty of this spiritual land's flora—from a simple offering of incense, petals, and lit candles on lily pads floating down the Ganges to elaborate wedding canopies. Blooms are also frequently referenced in traditional literature and poetry. People gather at bountiful markets featuring a kaleidoscope of fruits, vegetables, and packages of vibrant dyes, and where fragrant jasmine and brightly tinted yellow and orange marigold garlands, resembling pricey passementerie, are piled high. Indians embrace textiles with patterns that mimic nature. Cotton in rainbow colors is block-printed, tie-dyed, or embroidered with floral motifs and decorated with tiny mirrors. Cashmere shawls and silk saris have designs woven in stylized plant themes, in particular the paisley teardrop, which echoes the shape of the mango leaf.

Perhaps the best time to witness India's devotion to flowers is during a wedding ceremony. Marigolds, carnations, and roses cover a magnificently lush wedding canopy, called a *mandap*. The bride and groom wear garlands as part of their exquisite finery. Perfect for an engagement party, or any other special occasion, this joyous arrangement brims with parrot tulips, 'Léonidas' roses, sword bromeliad, cymbidium orchids, and croton leaves. The ceramic jug echoes the hues of the flowers.

INDIA'S CULTURAL DIVERSITY can be found in its outdoor markets where a multitude of dialects are spoken. Vendors carry everything, from exotic spices to eye-catching jewelry, some in the shapes of blossoms and petals, and enticing flowers. Shop ladies are happy to show you how to properly wrap a ravishing sari to achieve the perfect drape.

For weddings, floral-inspired henna designs decorate the bride's (and sometimes the groom's) hands and feet. This process, called *mehndi,* is a ceremony unto itself. The finished design is dabbed with lemon and sugar water to bring out the richness of the henna paste. Designs are also applied for other joyous occasions. After an artist completed amazing henna patterns on my hands, I asked, "Are you painting this design from something?" She replied, "Yes, from my heart." This dramatic arrangement of 'Léonidas' roses, marigolds, calla lilies, lotus pods, rose hips, and citronella leaves in a cheery, tangerine-ribbon-wrapped cylindrical vessel, surrounded by a sari, evokes the excitement and color of the enchanting Indian marketplace (see page 184 for complete instructions).

(TOP) I am enamored with Indian fashions. Their filigree-patterned brocades and tie-dyed textiles influence my flower arranging. From colorful embroidered sashes to stark-white Nehru collars, India's bold use of intricate design and distinctive silhouettes is a mainstay on most runways. I love collecting vintage Indian photographs, clustering a few together, and adorning them with sword bromeliad, 'Léonidas' roses, and a necklace of *rudraksha* prayer beads with tassels.

(ABOVE) Inspired by Indian miniatures, my painting of Ganesha seated in the lotus position on a lotus blossom incorporates the popular floral-paisley pattern. Prayers to this elephant god, one of the most recognizable and beloved deities of Hinduism, are thought to remove obstacles in one's life. (LEFT) India's roadside stalls abound with fragrant fruit. Get into the creative spirit and utilize fruit, such as oranges, as well as flowers and rose hips to create fabulous arrangements.

(RIGHT) Marigolds in hues of burnt orange and lemon yellow are abundant in India. Although mainly thought of as decorative plants, their flower heads are also used in many ceremonies, especially weddings. Made into garlands and offered to the gods and honored guests, they are also used to decorate the biers of the dead. Essential oils are extracted from marigolds for perfumes, and the flower itself acts as a repellent to pesty insects.

# The Colors

The colors of India are vivid. Saris, bangles, and turbans are available in as many gem tones as there are spices in a masala. Earth tones of mustard, curry, and cinnamon decorate pottery and textiles. Red is representative of passion and fertility as well as purity, and so is a popular choice for bridal dresses. Blue, the color of sea and sky, symbolizes calm and sincerity. Orange, gold, and saffron remind us of spring and sunshine. The greens of emeralds and pistachios are holy, while white symbolizes mourning. Holi, a festival of color held every spring, celebrates the fruitfulness of the land. Bonfires ward away evil spirits and negative energy. People throw packets of powders and liquid color at each other, and gifts of sweets and flowers are exchanged.

HOSPITALITY IS SYNONYMOUS with Indian culture. You might be surprised to receive an invitation to dine at the home of a mere acquaintance. Your host family will go out of its way to make you feel comfortable and welcome. I am always excited at the prospect of such an occasion, as I will surely be treated to a delicious meal. Indian cuisine, with its vast range of spices and herbs, is a match made in heaven for vegetarians. Indians pride themselves not only in the elaborate preparation of dishes with wonderfully robust flavors but also with their sumptuous display. There is always an immense array of chutneys, pickles, and yogurts accented with mint and cucumber. Flatbreads, or *naan*, and light, puffy *poori* breads are delectable replacements for the knife and fork, making it easy to scoop up curries and rice. Bowls of colorful chili peppers are always on hand for the adventurous. At traditional Indian meals, many dishes clutter the table so there is little room for large bouquets. A pristine water lily or peony floating in a transparent bowl of water will do the trick. Avoid any blooms that are too fragrant, as they may compete with the flavors of the food. If the meal is more formal, I often use the sideboard to display a more dramatic arrangement. In a high-ceilinged dining room, fill glass trumpet vases with blooming branches, such as quince, mixed with tuberose stalks that have a lovely fragrance. Hang bell votives from the limbs. Once lit, they illuminate the table and create a romantic ambience. The leafy canopy overhead is quite breathtaking, too.

(LEFT) Peonies, a favorite of Indians, are wonderful, dramatic flowers that symbolize prosperity and honor. Available in an array of luscious shades, peonies can stand alone, needing little else to complement their beauty. The addition of a few low-maintenance succulent flowers enhances them. I often use a colorful ceramic pitcher to showcase these gorgeous blooms. Place the arrangement on a beautiful piece of gold-threaded brocade, and you will dazzle everyone.

73

(RIGHT) I am always on the hunt for interesting alternatives to traditional vases. Here, I have used a metal cone made from a piece of vintage ceiling tin and filled it with white calla lilies, sweet tuberoses, and lilacs. Hang this delightful container from a silver ribbon in a guest room. The pleasant scents get stronger in the evening and your visitors will feel transported to an exotic land. (OPPOSITE) Serve perfumed tea in a whimsical Ganesha-shaped teapot accompanied by lotus-shaped accoutrements on a richly embellished white spread befit for a maharaja. Here, I have placed a white gardenia in a lotus pedestal dish. The lotus is a metaphor for India itself, symbolizing purity of heart.

N RECENT YEARS, the home-furnishings market has been greatly influenced by India's trademark decorative style. Furnishings and accessories are superbly handcrafted —from mirror frames with mother-of-pearl inlays to rope beds and silk lampshades. The multicolored patterned textiles that are quintessentially Indian are encrusted with sequins, reflective mirrored disks, seed pearls, and metallic thread work. These fabrics, often using flowers as a chief design motif, are fashioned into every imaginable domestic item, from curtains and pillows to bedspreads and linens. White, reminiscent of the Taj Mahal, is used to contrast with the bold colors. A traditional Indian home always includes a touch of colorful flowers to brighten even the most private spaces. Carved lattice screens provide the walls that are needed for a sanctuary, offering the feeling of retreating to a secluded ashram. An Indian teak daybed is a pretty focal point and the perfect romantic stage to showcase a mixture of pillows and a *kantha* quilt decorated with floral designs. Flowers should always be nearby as they can provide the path to enlightenment. Besides relaxation, use this personal space for the practice of yoga and other healing activities. Place a lotus flower on an altar to focus your mind and energy.

(OPPOSITE AND LEFT)
I love to create vignettes in a room setting. Old photographs and flea-market finds mixed with unique accessories, such as a Tantric bell, show your individuality. When I first came to New York, I would treat myself each week to a single, amazing flower, such as a succulent desert rose bud or a pastel pink peony. I always put it in a place of honor to meditate on its solitary beauty. At the time such purchases were considered luxuries, but they made me feel fulfilled.

For a special occasion, decorate your living room with a flower curtain that echoes the look of a traditional Indian garland. Here, I have strung carnation petals instead of the more commonly used marigold heads. This looks amazing in front of an antique settee upholstered in silk. Hang a favorite vintage photograph from a matching ribbon. Add embroidered pillows and throws to complete the rich, sophisticated look.

79

Pink is India's staple color—a favorite for fashion and home furnishings. Phalaenopsis orchids come in dozens of patterns and colors. Often in white or fuchsia, they can be spotted and freckled with intricate markings. Orchids are quite dramatic in their tall plant form or even as cut stems. Plucked petals dropped into a soothing bath and sprinkled atop a bed are perfect accents for a romantic evening. Votive candles complete the mood.

# Japanese Kimono

JAPAN IS A COUNTRY OF CULTURAL CONTRASTS—EXOTIC, SHY GEISHA PEEKING

FROM BENEATH COLORFUL PARASOLS WALK ALONGSIDE HIP YOUTH WITH THEIR CELL

PHONES CONSTANTLY ABUZZ. WHAT UNITES THESE TWO EXTREMES IS A SHARED

REVERENCE FOR THE UNLIMITED WONDERS OF NATURE. FLOWERS ARE CELEBRATED

EVERYWHERE—FROM LANDSCAPES DEPICTED ON SILK KIMONO AND SCROLL

PAINTINGS TO MURAKAMI'S "FLOWER BALLS" AND CUTE HELLO KITTY DAISIES.

# The Inspirations

Japanese style is all about subtlety and restraint. This understated elegance is best seen in the picturesque temples and shrines, regal palaces, contemplative gardens, and traditional pagodas of Kyoto. The exquisite craftsmanship and purity of form of these historic monuments is legendary. Classic interiors are typically devoid of decoration, yet are serene and dignified. The simple lines of sliding shoji screens made of paper panels, tatami mats, and low furniture create a calming and welcoming ambience. For me, the Ryōan-ji garden, with its carefully selected rocks and raked sand symbolizing the islands and surrounding ocean waves, is indicative of the Japanese philosophy that less is more. These abstract sculptural forms and textured patterns are illustrative of the attempt for perfection.

Panoramic views of mist-shrouded mountains and tranquil gardens, with walking stones and curved wooden bridges, are characteristic of this breathtaking land. Serene scenes of springtime's quintessential cherry blossoms are a delight to the senses. So, too, are the delicate flowers associated with this floating world—from elegant poppies, playful chrysanthemums, and delicious quince branches to the varied green shades of moss, grasses, and majestic bamboo stalks. One of my favorite blooms is the exquisite peony. A pair of these fragrant flowers carefully balanced on the edge of a shallow bamboo bowl, like chopsticks lain against their rest, creates a Zen mood.

A LESSON CAN be learned from the Japanese about how to savor each moment and enjoy the process. Westerners, so used to instant gratification, miss the joy and satisfaction of the gift of preparation. Every package is exquisitely wrapped, whether it is a present or a purchase from the marketplace. Old calligraphy books are hand-bound in rice paper and silk. The Japanese tenets of care and precision should also be applied to flower arranging. To create a gorgeous array of peonies, cover a plain glass vessel with delicate wrapping paper and attach black and red silk ribbons.

The simplest task has tremendous thought and pageantry behind it. When Westerners want a spot of tea, we tend to toss a tea bag hurriedly into any old mug. We are lucky if there is a wedge of lemon. In contrast, the Japanese have an elaborate, methodical, and unrushed ritual. How delightful to think about taking a refreshing pause in our hectic and noisy day. Refined over centuries, the Japanese tea ceremony and the art of flower arranging are enduring traditions.

(BELOW) During the Japanese tea ceremony, serenity is achieved through the ritual cleansing of utensils and the formal presentation of beautiful pottery and teapots. *Chabana* is the style of floral composition used in this ceremony. A simple, single branch of blossoms is placed in a tall bamboo, ceramic, or metal container.

(TOP) Geisha embody Japanese cultural tradition. They live in houses called *okiya*, or "flower towns." These entertainers wear silk kimono, often with elaborate floral motifs, *zori* or *geta* shoes outdoors, and split-toed socks, called *tabi*, indoors. Their payment, known as the "flower fee," is measured by the burning of an incense stick. (BOTTOM) It is customary in Japan to remove shoes before entering a home. Sandals, along with socks, are often provided for guests.

(RIGHT) Shades of white are appropriate for a Zen-like arrangement. Although this color symbolizes mourning in Japan, it evokes purity to Westerners. Here, I have filled a glass cylinder vase, covered in Japanese paper, with white roses, peonies, scabiosa, and calla lilies. Lemon leaves have been added to make the whites appear brighter. A wide strip of ribbon, representing an obi, has been tied around the vessel (see page 184 for complete instructions).

# The Colors

Japan's color palette covers the spectrum—from delicate yellows, pinks, and violets, to shades of green and red. Deep blue and white is a favorite color combination, and is often selected for textiles and porcelain. The ubiquitous peony exudes femininity, and comes in various lipstick colors—from pale pink to dark merlot. The floral design on a geisha's elegant kimono often corresponds to the changing seasons. Typically, in the spring, they are decorated with cherry blossoms or butterflies, and in the winter, bamboo or plum blossoms. A brilliantly colored obi is the finishing touch. There is also a neutral, tea-inspired palette of browns, amber, terra-cotta, and celadon. These colors look amazing next to the dark gloss of black or red lacquerware, especially with bold metallic accents of gold, silver, and bronze.

APANESE HOSPITALITY STRIVES for elegance and tranquility. Many houses are small, so entertaining often takes place in restaurants. Guests are greeted with an honorable bow as a sign of respect. Hosts are often given a small present to show gratitude for the invitation. Meals traditionally begin with the expression "*Itadakimasu*" (Japan's version of "*Bon appétit*"), a gracious way to offer thanks to those involved in its preparation. For me, the perfect Japanese food is sushi. I enjoy the contrasting flavors and textures as well as the artful arrangement. The various proteins layered with rice, wrapped in seaweed, and adorned with colorful salmon roe resemble tiny gifts waiting to be opened.

The table is an integral part of mealtime. Most are made of beautiful wood or stone so it is unnecessary to conceal the top with a tablecloth. Bamboo mats protect the surface and create a simple backdrop for place settings. Special accoutrements are implemented—sake cups, lacquer trays, and *bento* boxes. Most serving pieces are devoid of decoration, although some have flourishes of gold flecks or mother-of-pearl inlays. Whether designing a tabletop for an intimate gathering or a large-scale event, my philosophy is always the same: Knowing when to stop is a critical part of the creative process. Eliminating all that is superfluous is emblematic of the Japanese way of life. Rather than a frilly centerpiece, capture the essence of Japan by filling delicate vessels with understated displays. Arrange each bloom randomly as if it were still in the garden. Many flowers are so breathtakingly complex that there is no need to add anything extra.

(LEFT) Here, I have mimicked the delightful little morsels of a Japanese *bento* box with flowers. Single jewel-like blossoms of peonies, anemones, calla lilies, lisianthus, and cornflowers are wrapped in leaves that have been tied with raffia. Place them on a lacquer tray for a fun and delectable-looking sushi party centerpiece. It will surely make guests smile.

91

(LEFT) For a strong floral statement, pack rose heads of the same color into a lacquer or plain wood box. Arrange them in perfect rows. (OPPOSITE) When selecting a vase, look no further than nature itself—green bamboo makes the ideal vessel. Line several on a grass-cloth runner placed down the center of the table. Fill them with lotus pods, poppies, fiddlehead ferns, lady's slippers, and oncidium orchids, and a variety of eye-catching onion stalks, sea grapes, and selloum philodendron leaves.

(LEFT) Japan is known for origami, the ancient art of folding decorative paper to create ornate, whimsical objects. These vases, mimicking origami's precise creases, need just a few leaves of bamboo. (OPPOSITE) Set a stack of square plates on a pleated, palm-leaf place mat. This layered surface provides a wonderful canvas for displaying a single blossom under a butterfly-shaped dish. Add a color-coordinated dipping bowl. Bamboo chopsticks, tucked into a folded cloth napkin, complete the ensemble. Choose a stylish, yet practical, chopstick rest. It can be as simple as a small, polished river rock.

OR A JAPANESE-INSPIRED home, open spaces with clean lines and natural light are essential. Shoji screens, made of wooden fretwork and translucent rice paper called *washi*, are found in almost every house in Japan. They function as room dividers and sliding doors. Rice paper is also employed for lanterns to create a diffuse and soft glow. Fabric curtains are seldom used. Instead, paper, bamboo, and tatami reeds cover windows for privacy. Floors are left bare to create a spare look.

Uncluttered rooms not only enable your surroundings to breathe but they also allow you to appreciate the beauty of each object. *Wabi-sabi* is the Japanese word for the reverence of the natural aging of both living beings and things. Select furnishings or accessories with a patina, such as a cracked rakuware vase. Bring in bamboo stalks or a meticulously manicured bonsai tree. Be inspired by *ikebana*, the traditional art of Japanese flower arranging. Just a few blooms, twigs, and curled leaves are used to create a triangular-shaped composition. The three points of this geometric form can represent heaven, earth, and man, or the sun, moon, and earth. Apply these principles of harmony to achieve a tranquil environment.

Place a beautiful arrangement of cherry blossom branches in a tall, slender vase wrapped in decorative rice paper. Add a black and gold ribbon tied around the vessel as an accent. To achieve a contemporary look, use a colorful sheet of Japanese newspaper. A miniature Zen garden can easily be created by surrounding the floral composition with smooth river rocks.

97

Lady's slippers are so breathtakingly lovely. Don't use filler leaves because they will pollute the slender silhouette. Here, the flowers are placed in a textured, white vase. A leaf wrapped around the stalks, just above the lip of the container, has been secured with raffia. For a finishing touch, set the arrangement on a large leaf with variegated markings.

98

# Mexican
## Altar

WHEN I THINK OF MEXICO, WHAT COMES TO MIND IS A RELIGIOUS CELEBRATION.
THIS COUNTRY'S MOST BELOVED SPIRITUAL ICON, THE VIRGIN OF GUADALUPE, IS PRESENT
EVERYWHERE—IN HOMES AND CHURCHES, AND AT FESTIVALS. HER IMAGE IS
TRADITIONALLY SURROUNDED BY OFFERINGS OF CANDLES, HOLY WATER, AND FLOWERS.
THE JOYOUS COLORS OF THESE ROSES EVOKE THE ESSENCE OF THE MEXICAN SPIRIT.

# The Inspirations

Mexico's landscape is composed of contrasts—from the high Sierra Madres to hills dotted with coconut palms near the coast to the sparkling beaches close to the Mayan ruins of the Yucatán peninsula. Examples of delightful folk art are found everywhere. Ranging from embroidered textiles, pottery, and geometric-patterned tiles to naive paintings, handblown glass, and silver, their charming look enlivens the Mexican home. Many are decorated with floral motifs, evocative of the brilliant blooms that emblazon the traditional courtyard. This Oaxacan carving of a bull's head, reminiscent of an expressive Mexican mask, is adorned with a bouquet of roses in earthy tones.

Religious Mexicans offer petitions to a saint to gain help with the trials and tribulations of life. When these prayers are answered, portraits of the Virgin Mary and other popular saints are painted on wood, copper, or tin. Called retablos, these devotional paintings are often displayed at church shrines and in homes. Much like a gift of flowers, this time-honored folk art is a form of gratitude. Ex-votos, paintings depicting situations when a revered saint liberated the artist, family member, or friend from a difficult situation, include written descriptions of the event. *Milagros*, or miracles, are little amulets that are made of tin or aluminum. These inexpensive talismans, often in the form of animals or body parts, are believed to promote health and prosperity.

FLOWERS ARE AN integral part of Mexico, from daily life to feasts and religious holy days. A red rose petal is a cherished symbol of admiration that represents the mysteries of the human heart. This heart-shaped tin ornament is a popular token of love, much like a sweet bouquet. The Spanish inscription on its hand-embossed surface—*tu corazón siempre junto al mio*—translates as "your heart is always together with mine." I love collecting these small metal hearts to use as ornaments on my Christmas tree. Another popular Mexican decoration for this holiday and other occasions is the piñata, a brightly colored crepe-paper container, filled with toys and candy. Traditionally in the form of animals and stars, they now come in many shapes, including flowers. Wish your loved ones a *"Feliz Navidad"* with the gift of joyful blooms. Dress up the arrangement with a multi-colored ribbon tied around a ceramic vase. For a special touch, thread a hand-crafted ornament onto it. This present for the recipient's evergreen tree will be enjoyed for years.

(LEFT) My favorite artist, Frida Kahlo, often adorned her hair with roses. In honor of this flora- and fauna-lover, place tiny matchboxes, decorated with her self-portraits, in glazed pottery. (BELOW) I am not usually a fan of faux blooms, but these Mexican paper flowers are delightfully irresistible. For affordable dinner party decor, scatter bunches all over the table. Or, arrange them in ceramic vases for bursts of color.

(RIGHT) Old-fashioned flowers, such as carnations and marigolds, can take on a new sophistication when similar hues are clustered together. To create an arrangement with Mexican flavor, choose carnations in shades of pink and tangerine, and place them in a distressed tin. The trick to making these ruffled, once-passé blooms look modern is to group them tightly together (see page 185 for complete instructions).

# The Colors

The vitality and sheer magic of Mexican culture is expressed through the bold and effervescent use of joyful color. Renowned twentieth-century Mexican architect Luis Barragán incorporated this exuberance in his buildings, with their wide swaths of unadulterated pigments. Fiery red, tangerine, azure, turquoise, purple, lemon, lime, and dusty pink—these passionate colors are applied to everything with the same gusto as the spices that flavor the cuisine. These saturated hues are offset with earthy tones and whites. Mexican celebrations are an invitation to show off an array of colorful flowers. In homage to this country's strong affinity for color, cluster a dozen *botanica* candles in a spectrum of dazzling hues in the center of a rustic table. Fill pitchers with brilliant flowers and you are ready for a fiesta.

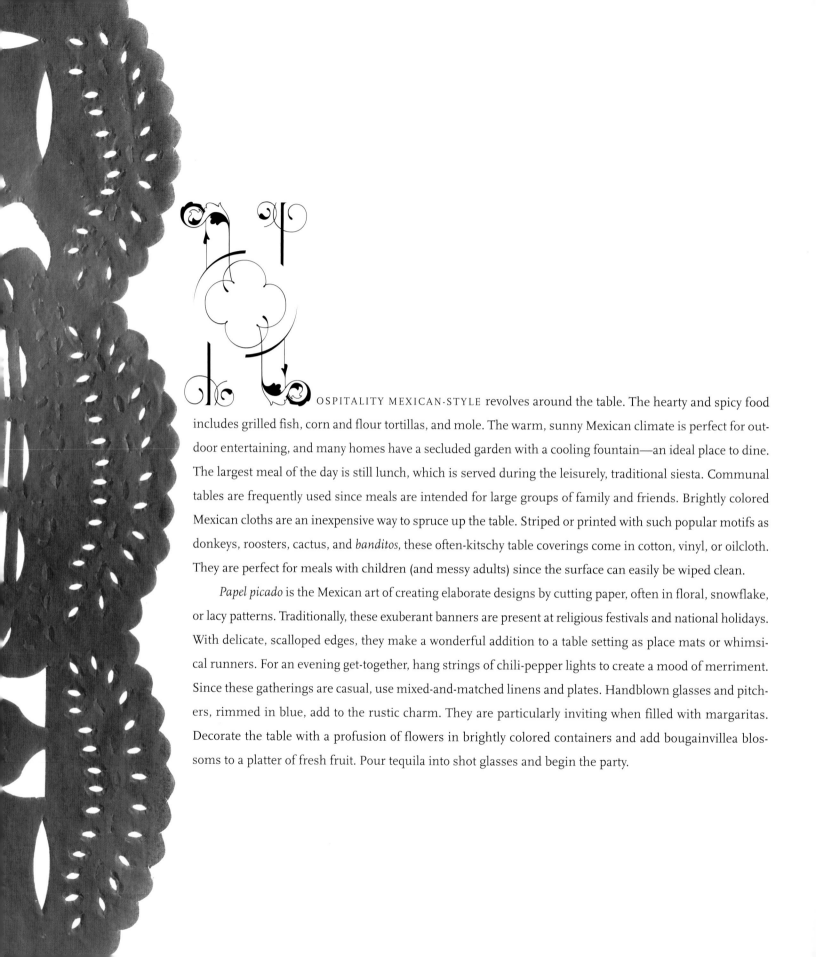

OSPITALITY MEXICAN-STYLE revolves around the table. The hearty and spicy food includes grilled fish, corn and flour tortillas, and mole. The warm, sunny Mexican climate is perfect for outdoor entertaining, and many homes have a secluded garden with a cooling fountain—an ideal place to dine. The largest meal of the day is still lunch, which is served during the leisurely, traditional siesta. Communal tables are frequently used since meals are intended for large groups of family and friends. Brightly colored Mexican cloths are an inexpensive way to spruce up the table. Striped or printed with such popular motifs as donkeys, roosters, cactus, and *banditos*, these often-kitschy table coverings come in cotton, vinyl, or oilcloth. They are perfect for meals with children (and messy adults) since the surface can easily be wiped clean.

*Papel picado* is the Mexican art of creating elaborate designs by cutting paper, often in floral, snowflake, or lacy patterns. Traditionally, these exuberant banners are present at religious festivals and national holidays. With delicate, scalloped edges, they make a wonderful addition to a table setting as place mats or whimsical runners. For an evening get-together, hang strings of chili-pepper lights to create a mood of merriment. Since these gatherings are casual, use mixed-and-matched linens and plates. Handblown glasses and pitchers, rimmed in blue, add to the rustic charm. They are particularly inviting when filled with margaritas. Decorate the table with a profusion of flowers in brightly colored containers and add bougainvillea blossoms to a platter of fresh fruit. Pour tequila into shot glasses and begin the party.

(LEFT) These tin cans, painted with wonderful images of the ever-popular Our Lady of Guadalupe, have been repurposed as vases. Each is filled with a different monochromatic bunch of sweetheart roses that echo the vessels' many colors. For your Mexican-themed party, place a row of them on your bathroom or bedroom windowsill. Intersperse them with votive candles in honor of the Virgin.

(LEFT AND RIGHT)
Countless vessel possibilities exist for sexy floral displays. Poppies in shades of orange are perfect in a blue Fiestaware tumbler, while a glazed water pitcher can double as a vase. Mercury glass hurricane lamps not only look attractive on a table but are also practical for entertaining outdoors.

(FOLLOWING PAGE)
Ceramics in a refreshing color combination of pomegranate red and lime green create a table setting as inspiring as a Diego Rivera still-life painting. 'Black Magic' and 'Supergreen' roses, bordered with hypericum berries and hydrangeas, echo the perky colors.

RADITIONAL MEXICAN HOUSES, with their painted stucco walls, terra-cotta planters, and clay tiles, set a picture-perfect stage for an extravaganza of flowers. Due to the agreeable climate, light-filled residences include shady court-yards and cool patios replete with stone fountains and reflecting pools. The cozy interiors are filled with textiles in wonderful color combinations, pottery often decorated with cheerful floral motifs, and hand-painted rustic furniture.

It is so simple to capture a Mexican mood in your home—just make sure that flowers are always present. Adorn an entrance hall table with bougainvillea and jacaranda branches. *Talavera* ceramic jugs of varying sizes make terrific vessels for roses. Place a single gerbera daisy in an old iridescent bottle on your bedside table. Set out a bowl piled high with fragrant lemons and their leaves alongside a lit candle on a wide bathtub ledge. Jazz up a tiled kitchen windowsill or wall niche with dahlias cra-dled in wooden or copper bowls from the Mexican marketplace. In the garden, weave a sweet-scented flowering vine through a trellis. String a rainbow-colored cotton hammock in the back-yard, and use glazed pots full of zinnias or impatiens as terrace borders or to define a romantic garden path.

Mexican folk-art furniture in miniature provides useful surfaces for stacks of cookbooks in the kitchen or potted, fragrant flowers in the bathroom. This charming child's chair, with its woven rush seat, is decorated with delightful, hand-painted rosebuds and petals. A hand-tied bouquet of ranunculus blooms has been placed atop it. These lovely flowers echo the designs on the chair.

115

Distressed Mexican furniture adds charm and zest to indoor or outdoor rooms. These crudely constructed wooden pieces are often painted in delightful hues, creating a perfect backdrop for fresh floral arrangements. Drape a serape or woven blanket over a hand-painted chair or a bench with a scalloped backboard that complements these bright carnations.

(RIGHT AND OPPOSITE)
Mexico's Day of the Dead, or *El Día de los Muertos*, is an annual festival honoring the deceased. Many families construct a home altar and decorate it with sugar skulls, skeletons, and marigolds. Flower petals are scattered outdoors to help the departed souls find their way back home. Assemble your own shrine in shades of white. Calla lilies are my choice flower for these memorials.

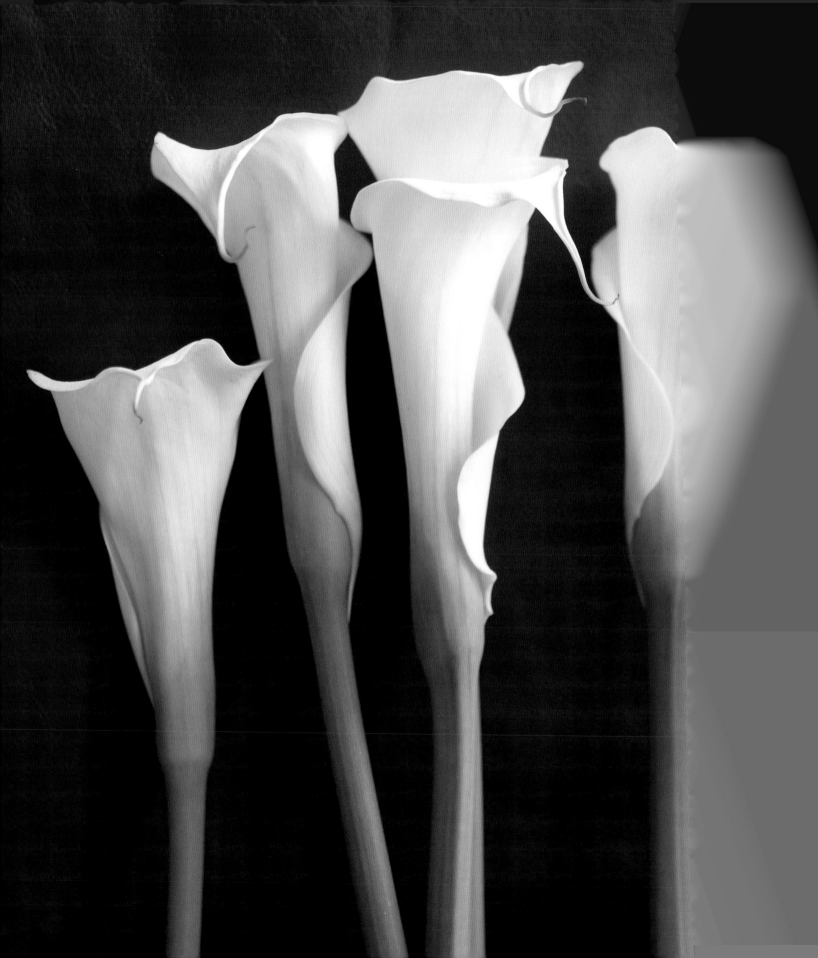

# Moroccan
## Medina

LOCATED ON THE NORTHERNMOST TIP OF AFRICA, MOROCCO IS AN INTOXICATING

MIX OF FRENCH, SPANISH, ARAB, AND BERBER CULTURES. ITS TERRAIN IS VARIED. ONE MOMENT

YOU ARE GAZING UP AT THE SNOW-CAPPED HIGH ATLAS MOUNTAINS, THE NEXT ONTO

A SCENE FROM *ARABIAN NIGHTS*—A CRESCENT MOON SHINING OVER THE SAHARA DESERT.

IF ONLY I COULD SPEND "A THOUSAND AND ONE NIGHTS . . ."

# The Inspirations

The hauntingly beautiful sounds of *adhan*, or the call to prayer, echo across Morocco. Practiced five times daily, it is the perfect soundtrack to this mysterious land. The country's imperial cities, rich tapestries of culture and beauty, are Casablanca, Meknes, Rabat, Fez, and Marrakech, known as the "Red City" because of its many terra-cotta buildings. Souks, shopping areas in a town's medina, or ancient quarter, explode with exotic goods and traditional crafts. The air is filled with the aroma of pungent spices. The crowded and dusty marketplace is brimming with storytellers, snake charmers, and camels. Seated on kilim rugs, women apply *mehndi*, ornate decorations often with floral motifs, on palms and feet.

One night after leaving my hotel in Marrakech, I was brought into the heart of the medina for dinner. On the dark street an elderly man in traditional dress greeted me. Holding a pierced-metal lantern, he led me through a large, nail-studded wooden door to a beautiful courtyard restaurant. I felt as if I had arrived on a magic carpet. Seated at a table, scattered with rose petals and sequins, I was presented with a brass hand-washing basin filled with marigold blossoms. What followed was an enchanting evening of great food, drinks, music, and belly dancing. My journey through Morocco was transformative and has inspired my floral designs.

CLASSIC MOROCCAN towns are comprised of mosques, fountains, *hammams, riads,* a medina, and a souk. The mosque's minarets are the town's dominating architectural feature. Colorful tiled fountains are typically found in gardens, their octagonal shape symbolic of cosmic order and balance. The water is a cooling respite from the desert heat. The *hammam,* or Turkish bath, is a mainstay in Islamic culture. It is not only the place to purify the body before religious services but it also functions as a social gathering spot. Opulent *riads,* with rhythmically repetitive decorative details, have airy courtyards. The souk, or marketplace, located in the medina, is charged with energy and exuberance, where bartering is a much-anticipated activity rooted in the culture. I revive dreams of Morocco by creating perfumed arrangements. Here, inspired by the colorful, local spices, I have combined lemon branches and 'Red Robin' photinia foliage with 'Gold Strike' roses and vanda orchids. They are displayed in a terra-cotta pot atop a table covered with a coarsely woven rug (see page 186 for complete instructions).

(BELOW) In this exotic country, many women opt to wear the burqa or the hijab, traditional coverings. Conventional men's attire includes the djellaba, a hooded, long-sleeved cotton garment with intricate button closures at the neck. Here, a felt fez is perched on an antique brass candlestick, accented with a striped 'Shirley Temple' peony. A colorful Berber rug completes the vignette.

(TOP) A *riad*, a typical dwelling with a square central courtyard, is often festooned with brightly colored flowers such as hibiscus. (BOTTOM) Elaborate hand-cut tiles, or *zellij*, are used to adorn flooring, walls, fountains, and columns. These tiles are made into mosaics by piecing together glazed chips in geometric, interlocking patterns that are mesmerizing brainteasers.

(RIGHT) Cymbidium orchids, 'Léonidas' and 'Limona' roses, and hypericum berries fill a vase that has been sprinkled with glittering chips of mica. The arrangement which is on top of a multihued rug, has been placed in front of a rustic wooden shutter with wrought-iron handles that is parted, allowing light to stream in. This setting brings to mind a delightful, sunny day in Morocco.

126

# The Colors

Morocco has a distinctive color palette. Its countryside is ablaze with radiant shades of saffron, pink, and crimson in contrast to the parched, sandy desert. However, *bleu Majorelle,* or cobalt blue, is the color commonly associated with this land. It is reflective of the Mediterranean coast and the deep-blue sky. The gleaming, white-washed clay walls typical of Morocco are a stunning contrast to this bold hue. Doors and window shutters are often painted in luscious shades of tangerine orange, yellow, and pistachio green. Earth tones, like burnt sienna, terra-cotta, and chocolate brown, mimic the colors of loose spices sold in the souk. Embroidered textiles and rugs display such deep hues as plum, aubergine, and garnet red, while jewel-toned mint tea glasses, with metallic accents, exemplify this alluring culture.

127

ENTERTAINMENT IS A vital part of the Moroccan lifestyle. A buffet table, overflowing with delectable cuisine intermingled with fragrant flowers, creates a rich and glorious tableau. Hand-crafted metal and clay serving pieces are festive accents. *Tagines*, glazed earthenware vessels with conelike lids, are colorful and joyous. They are used for stewing chicken or lamb with vegetables, preserved lemons, almonds, and dried fruits. Star and crescent moon cutouts allow the spice-infused flavors to waft aromatically. Olives and dollops of yogurt are perfect condiments for mounds of couscous.

A favorite afternoon ritual is the drinking of refreshing green tea, which is served with mint leaves. Everyone takes a break to sip this sweet Moroccan specialty—the ideal digestive. Almond cookies, honey cake, and fruit salad are a favorite accompaniment. To enliven this pastime, add the natural touch of a single, cheerful blossom in a ceramic bud vase. For more formal occasions, tables are set with fine linens and silver candelabra. Banquettes and divans are upholstered in boldly patterned, flocked velvets. Seating becomes even more comfortable with the addition of throw pillows, covered with brocade that is decorated with floral motifs. Poufs made of woven textiles, leather, and damasks can be pulled around the table for extra seating. A courtyard is the perfect place to entertain, especially when the weather mimics the warm, dry North African climate. Surround yourself with potted palms and urns brimming with sun-drenched flowers and you will feel transported to a Moroccan oasis.

(LEFT) Here, a scattering of curry-colored pincushion protea flowers, in bright yellow glazed crockery of varying heights, interspersed among colorful earthenware *tagines* with their delightful conical lids, complements a Moroccan feast for the eyes.

129

Morocco has always been an artistic mecca for painters and writers drawn there for its brilliant light and exotic atmosphere. This cobalt-blue-and-white color scheme reflects the outdoor style of Mediterranean North Africa. A couch heaped with embroidered and tasseled pillows opposite silk-covered and leather poufs is welcoming for a relaxed snack of fruits, olives, and nuts. A low metal tray table has been covered with plates and serving pieces. The 'Casablanca' lilies in long-necked white vases in the center of the tray need little else to make a statement.

A silver tea table with decorative glasses and flower-topped stirrers are complemented by a pure white arrangement of cymbidium orchids and roses. Sprigs of mint complete the fresh and light look. The glass vase has been filled with sparkly stones that echo the sequined embellishments of the striped Riffian rug. A silvery leather pouf is the perfect height for the low table. These comfortable seats are chic in any decor—ethnic-inspired or modern.

OROCCAN INTERIORS ARE dramatic. The decor is a fusion of bright colors, textures, and artisan finishes—from cedar doors carved with intricate patterns of radiating stars to highly crafted bronze door knockers. Walls are often crisp and gleaming white, or polished plaster surfaces stained with colorful pigment, a technique know as *tadlekt*. Elaborately embroidered and woven textiles and layered rugs are used with abandon. A Moroccan daybed in ravishing silk brocade is perfect for lounging about in this serene environment. The placement of a cascade of creamy white and red rose petals atop a nearby mother-of-pearl inlaid stool adds to the dreaminess. Pairs of matched carved wooden chairs and leather-covered poufs in candy colors provide additional seating. Polychrome tile-lined walls with deeply set plaster niches and lacy cutouts continue the exotic look.

These airy rooms, embellished with arched doorways, beams, and cornices, spill out into the sun-drenched courtyard gardens. Outdoor spaces provide opportunities to be fanciful. A blue-domed gazebo is a delightful structure that offers protection from the brilliant sunshine. This intoxicating setting can be further spiced up with blooms and palms in Fez pottery.

Moroccan hexagonal and star-shaped lanterns look divine hanging in foyers, placed on rug-covered tables, or sitting on the floor. These silver and brass fixtures are paneled with clear and colored glass. If the lanterns are not electrified, use pillar candles to illuminate the space. Sprinkle fresh rose petals on surfaces to create a romantic mood. How enchanting!

(LEFT) A turquoise ceramic water pitcher filled with bright yellow 'Moonshine' achillea creates a festive Moroccan-inspired arrangement. (OPPOSITE) Here, at poolside, the marvelous Moroccan blue-and-white color scheme has been employed. Pierced, white ceramic ginger-jar lanterns are grouped with a Fez urn filled with sun-flowers— they are indeed inviting touches. The distinctive cobalt blue is attributed to Jacques Majorelle, a twenti-eth-century French artist who resided in Marrakech. His luxuri-ant garden abounded with palms and suc-culents. Fountains, doors, and even urns painted in the epony-mous blue shimmer through the greenery.

# Southern Roots

SOUTHERNERS ARE WONDERFULLY HOSPITABLE AND ECCENTRIC. LIKE THIS

DOLL-HEAD PORCELAIN VASE, LADIES OFTEN DON A LOVELY, FLOWER-EMBELLISHED

HAT REMINISCENT OF A BYGONE ERA WHEN GLOVES WERE DE RIGUEUR.

A SOUTHERN SOJOURN WILL REMIND YOU OF A TIME WHEN CHILDREN ANSWERED,

"YES, MA'AM" AND "YES, SIR" TO THEIR ELDERS. SUNDAYS ARE RESERVED

FOR CHURCH SERVICES, FOLLOWED BY LARGE, HOME-COOKED FAMILY FEASTS.

# The Inspirations

The South is my ancestral home. Recollections of relaxing on wide porches surrounded by white columns on moon-lit nights take me back there. A sense of timelessness is expressed in the stately houses decorated with chintz-covered, cozy furniture, lacy curtains, and floral wallpaper. These fine residences, filled with heirlooms, antique furnishings, and faded photographs, are the perfect setting for sweet-scented arrangements of flowers.

Growing up in rural Virginia, my playground was Grandfather's home, with its acres of vegetable and flower gardens. The landscape was bordered by rows of magnolia trees; their white blossoms filled the air with perfume. The house was miles away from neighbors, so my sister was my sole playmate. This bucolic property nourished my strong appreciation of nature. With fields of brilliant sunflowers and black-eyed Susans stretching toward the sun, it was never necessary to make a trip to the florist. Cutting gardens were filled with delphiniums, poppies, and foxgloves. Daily pickings were arranged in painted sap buckets and galvanized tins. The flowers were then transferred into our late grandmother's lovely vases and placed in every room. It was a nice way to surprise our family. Lazy summer days remind me of the delights of sharing sliced peaches, iced lemon cake, and sweet tea at picnics on the freshly mowed lawn. Southern charm is plentiful.

THE GLORY OF the Old South is rooted in the stylish capitals of Richmond, Charleston, New Orleans, Natchez, and Savannah. Thankfully, due to southerners' passion for the past, a gracious way of living has been preserved in these cities. If I had to use one word to epitomize the South, it would be *manners*. When a child questions, "But, why?" the response, in a slow southern drawl, is always the same: "Because it simply is not done."

Families and friends gather regularly, often sitting on the front veranda drinking sweet tea and watching the world go by. Porch swings replace the comforts of a sofa. Stories that have been told a million times before are still endearing. For those sticky, hot summer days when a little more kick is needed, mint juleps are served. The traditional silver cups, when not filled with the sugar, mint, and bourbon concoction, make lovely vessels to hold nosegays of cotillion-worthy garden roses. Or, bunches of daisies in old-fashioned double glasses are a way to create a lovely display. Such times conjure up the style and grace of the Old South.

(BELOW) For a romantic effect, dress up a garden tabletop with purple passion blooms. Set them on a plate and cover the composition with a vintage glass cloche.

(TOP) Sweet tea is the preferred refreshment throughout the South. Glass pitchers filled with this thirst-quenching drink are covered with crocheted lace doilies. A favorite pastime is to socialize with drink in hand on the porch—the South's version of the stoop. (BOTTOM) In the South, outdoor adventures abound. You can always find a swing hanging from a tree limb. Adorn it by wrapping flowering purple passion fruit vines around the aged ropes.

(LEFT) Joyous dahlias, only available during the summer, are a favorite. While they are in season, I always try to incorporate them in my arrangements. These wide-bloomed flowers, in a variety of oranges, reds, and yellows, require no other filler to create dramatic compositions. Brightly glazed ceramic water pitchers and creamers are wonderful alternatives to the traditional glass vase.

# The Colors

The spectrum of hues that one associates with the American South invites feelings of sultry languor. As the landscape is predominately shades of green, this color can be considered the perfect neutral. From the deepest chartreuse to the lightest celadon, green provides the backdrop for bold colors and subdued pastels alike. Pomegranate red, peachy coral, melon orange, and blush pink are choice warm colors that contrast nicely with burnished wood furnishings. Mixing flowers from a traditional cutting garden—poppies, delphiniums, foxgloves, sunflowers, and black-eyed Susans—creates an inimitable Southern bouquet. Hydrangeas, in delicate shades of white, lavender, pink, and periwinkle, soften pretty floral arrangements, as do creamy magnolia blossoms. Buttery yellows mimic the glow of the sun and make rooms cheerful. Tomato-red and lettuce-green bowls echo the palette of a vegetable garden.

145

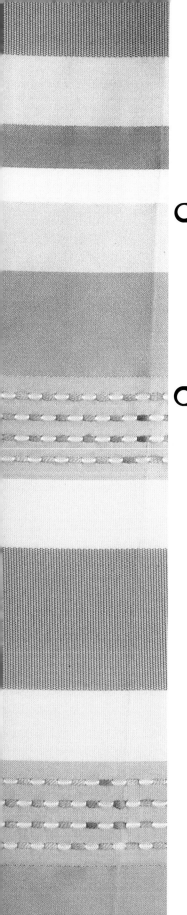

NTERTAINING HAS ALWAYS been an expression of hospitality throughout the South. The finest silver, china, and crystal stemware, passed down for generations, were often set on tables covered with hemstitched linen or lace cloths or stacked gracefully on a wooden sideboard. But though special occasions and holidays still call for elegance and gorgeous flower arrangements, rarely is such formality embraced today. Dinnertime was reserved for families to be together and discuss the day. My family enjoyed this tradition. The kitchen table was set beautifully, but in a more casual manner, with everyday china and glassware. (Father refused to drink from a plastic cup, saying that things did not taste the same as from a glass.) We honored this time together with a centerpiece bouquet of fresh-cut flowers from our garden. Mother made homemade biscuits and gravy to complement the entrée. We always left room for freshly baked berry pies and cobblers. A huge amount of work and love went into preparing this daily repast.

The "covered dish" meal, usually held after a church service, is considered the ultimate Southern entertaining experience. For these potluck gatherings, family and friends proudly present their best recipes. These dishes are artfully laid out on buffet tables. Fresh-cut flowers in simple pottery enhance the delectable display. Offerings of deviled eggs, potato and macaroni salads, and every casserole imaginable are shared. A separate dessert table holds banana pudding, egg custard, chess pie, and more home-baked goodies. Other parts of the South embrace smoked meats smothered in barbeque sauce, fried chicken, corn bread, heaping sides of collard greens and black-eyed peas, and, of course, yummy sweet potato pie.

(OPPOSITE) This pastel-striped silk taffeta, suitable for a gorgeous ball gown, would also make a beautiful table runner. In fact, the traditional drawing rooms of the South are decorated with such sumptuous materials as silk and satin—from draperies and tablecloths to upholstered settees covered with chintz throw pillows that echo the colors of the garden.

147

(LEFT) In this quaint farmhouse, a white wooden kitchen table is adorned with Ball canning jars overflowing with Queen Anne's lace, lisianthus, 'Sterling' roses, scabiosa, and blackberry and passion fruit stems. These glass containers are wonderful for showing off wildflower pickings. Purple vines of various shades add contrast. Snaking down the table, they create a natural runner. (OPPOSITE) A painted sap bucket takes the place of a glass vase. Stuffed with purple scabiosa, lisianthus, and variegated hydrangea, it adds a burst of color for a makeshift bar area. These simple arrangements possess rustic charm.

A Fourth of July picnic, Southern style, is set dockside. I have laid the table with red-and-white linens, white crockery, and wicker accessories. Bluish grapes complete the patriotic color scheme. Glazed pots are filled with dahlias.

151

(LEFT) Striped fabric napkins, tucked into a vintage picnic basket, are as American as apple pie. Gather small bunches of flowers together to create an instantly festive look. (OPPOSITE) Flashy, red-and-white variegated dahlias remind me of Independence Day fireworks. Ample stacks of plain white dishes are just right for fuss-free summer entertaining.

Southern Houses Range in style and scale from cottages and simple farmhouses to mansions. I fondly remember the more formal past, and I love the interiors of fancier houses with grand staircases that lead to opulent rooms for entertaining. Abundant floral arrangements on entrance tables welcome guests. The formal spaces have crystal chandeliers hanging regally from ceiling medallions surrounded by ornate plasterwork. Groupings of transferware plates are prominently displayed on intricately carved mantelpieces and antique furniture. Decorated with hand-painted wallpapers and toiles depicting pastoral scenes, these spaces are quintessentially Southern. Velvet and taffeta drapes frame windows and French doors, affording views of the landscape.

Whether cultivating a backyard cutting garden or an estate with formal plantings and manicured lawns, Southerners take their gardens—a badge of pride—seriously. Weeping willows and trees dripping with Spanish moss are surrounded by white picket fences or iron gates. Dogwood and magnolia trees pepper the landscape. Latticed gazebos and trellises provide a place for ivy and roses to climb. Viburnum, affectionately known as a snowball bush, is a prerequisite for every grandmother's lawn.

In a light-filled farm-house kitchen, deep- and pale-purple scabiosa, lisianthus, and variegated hydrangea blooms have been tightly arranged in a simple ceramic jug placed on a tray table (see page 186 for complete instructions). The green of the leaves and the nearby wine bottles offer a pleasant contrast to the feminine tones of the lavender-colored flowers. Surrounded by white pottery, they bring joy and color into the heart of the house.

A collection of milk-glass vessels in a variety of shapes and sizes line a white fireplace mantle. They provide the perfect spot for garden pickings of such lovely flowers as scabiosa, delphinium, and nigella. When cutting the stems, vary the heights for drama. An occasional blossom adds interest. This modern-day version of garniture captures the quirky, eccentric Southern sensibility.

# Tropical Rain Forest

UNDER THE RAIN FOREST'S HEAVY CANOPY EXISTS A PLETHORA OF EXOTIC
PLANTS AND CREATURES. ORCHIDS DRAPE THE TREES; SCATTERED LEAVES FORM
A SOFT CARPET. SHADES OF SCINTILLATING GREENS GO ON FOR MILES.
ANIMALS SNAP BRANCHES AND CALL OUT, LETTING US KNOW THAT THIS IS THEIR
WORLD, AS IT HAS BEEN SINCE THE BEGINNING OF TIME. THIS IS EDEN.

# The Inspirations

The world contains many rain forests, from the Amazon to the Asian tropics. Those of Costa Rica and Puerto Rico are particularly inspiring to me. These extraordinary verdant habitats are a botanist's paradise. This fragile ecosystem is replete with singing frogs, parakeets, parrots, toucans, hummingbirds, and butterflies. Its thriving depends on water—whether it is pounding against the beach, cascading down from a waterfall, or raining. Moisture is abundant, and the clear blue water contrasts beautifully with all the greenery.

The rain forest is the motherland of the "green" dream. This untamed and mysterious land contains a wealth of tropical leaves, mosses, and ferns in every shade. The textures and patterns of the leaves, ranging from deep ridges and contrasting stripes to filigreed veins, is artful. Inspiring plants include umbrella papyrus, banana and palm trees, as well as fiddlehead ferns. Vibrant, pastel orchids are rooted in tree trunks while orange palm dates hang from lush foliage, marking the landscape with unexpected color. Fragrance fills the air. This is my vision of the perfect world. When I see this natural bounty, I chuckle—being a floral designer, I know what fetches top dollar at the flower market. In the spirit of the rain forest, I have created a humble display of orange palm dates with a backdrop of grass skirting.

THE CULTURE OF the tropics embodies everyone's escapist fantasy—carefree living in this awe-inspiring, bounteous environment. Indoor and outdoor spaces are effortlessly combined by way of open pavilions and sheltered courtyards. Like a rain forest's canopy, covered decks and terraces provide protection from the elements. Functioning as "outdoor rooms," these structures also enable one to commune with nature. During a visit to the Costa Rican rain forest, each morning I was greeted by impish white-faced monkeys banging on my airy villa's windows, hoping that I had some tasty treats.

Holes are cut in ceilings and floors to welcome living plants. Beds are romantically shrouded with crisp, white netting woven of native materials. Fabrics, wall coverings, and flooring are eco-friendly. Tree trunks provide natural seating. To capture the cultural essence, consider hanging a string hammock in a breezy screened-in porch amid fan palms in colorful clay pots. Here, I have taken a simple coconut with sprouting leaves and placed it in a hammered metal basin to show off its quiet, refined beauty.

(TOP) A popular motif for textiles and wallpaper is tropical botanicals. These enchanting fabrics, from stylized ferns to exotic blossoms, are an emblematic feature of 1950s design that is still popular today. (BOTTOM) Botanical-inspired patterned wallpapers and fabrics with images of hibiscus, bamboo stalks, and palm and banana leaves are reminiscent of the "Tropicana" look of the Fifties. A dramatic and sculptural arrangement of feathery ferns and stalks of heliconia, which is sometimes mistaken for the more common bird-of-paradise, is straight out of the rain forest.

(ABOVE) A croton leaf with bright yellow veins complements a colorful still life, an oil painting of a coffee can.

163

(LEFT) Often flowers of the same genus have subtle variations of color, like these vanda orchids. Clustered together, they create unusual shape, depth, and texture. Fiddlehead ferns add contrast and whimsy. A hulled-out tree trunk is a quirky and organic vase in keeping with the rain forest theme.

# The Colors

The native color palette of the rain forest is every shade of green known to man—from yellow-hued chartreuse to the bluish green found in the undergrowth. The velvety, rich, dark soil and ancient bark of the looming trees are counterpoints to the dominant emerald greens. It is impossible to ignore the brilliant tones of the exotic flora that mingle with all this greenery. Tropical flowers in startlingly vibrant yellow, orange, crimson, and purples—in shades of lavender to the deepest eggplant—abound among neutral-colored stalks and branches. The blazing equatorial sun magnifies the bold plumage of the native birds. For a beautiful effect, cluster together little green vases, some filled with a vanda orchid bud. As the finishing touch, add a huge elephant ear leaf for a striking backdrop.

FOR ENTERTAINING THAT evokes the feeling of the tropical rain forest, there is one rule: Keep it simple. The way of life in these extremely humid climates is informal, yet exotic. When preparing for a "green"-themed party, your design should reflect this naturalistic look. Enjoy transforming your home into paradise. Infuse the spaces with untamed energy—bright feathers, elephant ear leaves, and bird-of-paradise flowers provide whimsical and unexpected flourishes. Many tropical blossoms grow on large stalks and are too tall for centerpieces. Pluck their blooms and float them in glass cubes. For an outdoor evening celebration, set a table under a garden canopy or trellis. To create a lighthearted mood, the host and hostess should wear simple hibiscus blooms tucked behind their ears. Welcome each guest with a handblown glass overflowing with a syrupy concoction of dark rum and ripe banana. Garnish zesty cocktails and nonalcoholic juices with star fruit wedges and flower petals. Serve hors d'oeuvres on straw trays layered with oversize leaves and a sprinkling of orchid heads for beauty.

If you are entertaining in the city, bring the spirit of the jungle inside. Place a plush emerald-green runner on a long wood table to mimic moss. Or leave the table au naturel. Finish the look with grass place mats, woven linens, and wood-handled utensils. Serve buffet or family style. To conserve space on the table, I use single flowers rather than overly large arrangements. Put tall tropical flowers, such as orchids, in individual glass vases by each place setting. Offer platters of plantains and grilled fish atop large leaves. Finish the meal with a delicious *torta tres leches* (three-milk cake) and decorate each dessert plate with an edible petal or two.

For a naturalistic place setting, choose serving vessels, stemware, and plates with organic shapes. I use china in earthy-brown tones and add a matching Russel Wright water pitcher. Natural-fiber textiles, such as cotton, straw, burlap, or jute, contribute to this distinctive look. Fresh palm leaves make the perfect plate liners, and a single fiddlehead fern tucked into each napkin adds playful humor.

167

(PREVIOUS PAGE) For this rain forest-themed tabletop, I mixed vintage and modern glasses and ceramics in shades of green. Lovely stems of cymbidium and dendrobium orchids and lady's slippers have been interspersed with woody lanuginose and lotus pods. Leafy umbrella papyrus and eucalyptus have been added for height and drama. The communal table is set with Russel Wright china atop a vintage retro-printed textile. (LEFT AND OPPOSITE) Having three stalks' of the same tropical flower, such as cymbidium or dendrobium orchids, or lady's slippers, and a bunch of niganosa, in a single vase, allows your guests to study the beauty of these beautiful blooms.

(RIGHT) A colorful coffee can is filled with bunches of 'Léonidas' and 'Jade' roses, ranunculus, protea, mango calla lilies, and Billy's buttons. It is the perfect vessel to capture the spirit that permeates the rain forest. Lady's mantle and hypericum berries are added for contrast. An elephant ear leaf placed behind is a fun, natural foil (see page 187 for complete instructions). (OPPOSITE) This hand-tied bouquet of arum lilies, 'Jade' roses, skimmia, and brunia berries bordered with coconut bark sits languorously on a sheet of faux-wood wallpaper.

S OME OF THE plants and flowers from the rain forest are quite large and create amazing impact through scale. Their grand proportions are well suited to sleek, minimalist home interiors. Place variegated philodendron (known as elephant ears) and palm fronds in tall, cylindrical, clear glass vases. Medium-size to large stones serve as a decorative weight, holding the containers down. Or, set a ponytail palm tree in a terra-cotta pot in a spare corner. The umbrella-like foliage springing from the bending trunk is chic and sculptural. Wild and exotic flower arrangements add a tropical touch to an urban setting. The intriguing shapes of such blooms as bird-of-paradise flowers, with their strong lines and patterns, look striking against a plain, monochromatic backdrop.

To capture a paradisiacal vision, add botanical patterned wallpapers and fabrics to the design scheme. As tropical flowers and leaves make a strong statement, stick to naturalistic silhouettes and bold colors. This bunch of green bananas is an eye-catching sculpture. The eggplant-colored floret will bloom before perishing. Place the tableau on a wooden pedestal atop a rustic side table. It makes an exotic conversation piece. Add a 'Tying Shin Grace' phalaenopsis orchid head to evoke paradise.

Though green is the dominant color of the rain forest, flowers such as cymbidium orchids in various shades of pink and eggplant can also be found there. Limiting them to monochromatic tones of pink or purple allows your eye to focus on the proportion, line, and scale of over-the-top blooms. Groupings of cymbidium orchids, fiddlehead ferns, 'Safari Sunset' leucadendron, black calla lilies, brunia, red skimmia, and succulents placed in gourd-shaped vessels look weird and wonderful.

177

# PRIMER

# GUIDELINES

## FOR CREATING AND MAINTAINING FLORAL ARRANGEMENTS

SIMPLE FLORAL COMPOSITIONS are timeless. I strive for arrangements that are as natural looking as possible. Always keep in mind the fundamentals of flower arranging—texture, color, contrast, and balance—to produce a harmonious and artful creation.

Begin by purchasing flowers or picking them from the garden. If you are gathering flowers from outdoors, collect them in the morning before the blooms open. Immediately after cutting, place them in a pail or a galvanized florist bucket filled with room-temperature water. If you are buying flowers, choose a reputable florist or retailer. Don't be afraid to ask about care and longevity, and make sure to recut the stems of purchased flowers when you get home. Most fresh blooms should last around five days.

Preparing and arranging flowers can be a dirty affair. Always protect your work surface. Before making a floral composition, remove all leaves and thorns that will be below the water level as they will decay and make the water slimy. Always use room-temperature water when handling flowers. Cold water will shock them and they will perish faster. Certain flowers, such as hydrangea, lilacs, and viburnum, should also be spritzed, as they drink from their blooms as well as from their stems. Many tropical flowers have a sticky residue on their surface. To remove it, wash the bloom using a plant mister, or dunk the flower in water, and let it dry.

### FLOWER ARRANGING EQUIPMENT

This equipment list highlights my preferred tools. As I don't believe in using wires to prop up flowers, you will not find wire here.

### CONTAINERS

Choosing a container is an enjoyable part of arranging flowers. Don't settle for a conventional plain glass vase. Experiment with glass bottles and vintage cups. For inspired arrangements, seek vessels from around the world. Make sure that your containers are spotlessly clean as bacteria can harm flowers.

### FLORAL CLIPPERS, FLORAL KNIFE, AND LEAF STRIPPER

Floral clippers and a floral knife are used to prepare flowers for arranging, including stripping away leaves and trimming stems. A leaf stripper is another option, but if not used properly, it can break the stems. Handle your tools with care, and always keep them clean and dry. Maintaining a sharp blade ensures a clean cut. Never use paper or fabric scissors to trim flowers; a dull blade can compress the stems and prevent adequate hydration.

Floral clippers are the better tool for cutting thicker-stemmed flowers. However, a floral knife is preferable for producing a sharp angle when cutting woody-stemmed blooms, such as roses. Some stalk-stemmed flowers, such as amaryllis, should be slashed three to four times at the base of each stem to create numerous pathways through which the flower can drink. The thick, branchlike stems of certain flowers, such as hydrangea, should also be smashed at their ends with a hammer so that more water reaches the blooms.

### FLORAL FOAM

Floral foam comes in many shapes and sizes, from bricks to cones. Oasis is my preferred brand as it absorbs water quickly (between thirty seconds and two minutes depending upon the size of the piece). Less expensive foams take more time to become fully sat-

urated with water. Also, they may clog the stems of flowers and prevent them from hydrating. Either place the foam in your container before adding water or presoak it in a bucket. Cut flower stems at a sharp angle that will pierce the foam easily. Be aware that floral arrangements in a foam base will not last as long as those in water. Do not reuse the foam as it will fail to hold water a second time.

### FLORAL WATER TUBES

Some flowers, such as ranunculus, have thin stems that easily break when being inserted into foam. Floral water tubes will help to protect delicate stems and allow for easier manipulation. They are useful for tight arrangements. The tubes can also be used to lengthen shorter-stemmed blooms.

Fill the tube with room-temperature water and place the pierced rubber cap on top. If the stem is too thick to fit through the cap hole, expand the hole using a floral knife. Carefully place the flower stem through the cap. The tube's spiked bottom will allow for easy penetration of the foam. Make sure that the tube is hidden by greenery or flowers. It is important to place poisonous flowers, such as daffodils, in water tubes. This provides the

stems with individual water sources, which allows them to be safely included in mixed floral bouquets.

### PLASTIC LINERS

Clear plastic liners keep containers from leaking. They come in a variety of sizes and can be easily cut with scissors for a perfect fit. Liners are available at most floral supply and craft shops as well as at gardening and hardware stores. If you cannot find a plastic liner in the appropriate size for your container, use a single, seamless cellophane sheet. Trim any visible cellophane.

### OTHER USEFUL ITEMS:

Double-sided tape, green floral tape, plant mister, raffia

### MAKING FLOWER ARRANGEMENTS LAST

Keep your flowers looking fresh by frequently changing the water. Add flower food to the water as it encourages buds to develop and contains antibacterial agents. A cool room is ideal for cut flowers. Avoid placing an arrangement in direct sunlight or in a drafty spot. These guidelines also apply to plant care. Many plants, such as orchids, adapt to their environment and do not like to be moved.

# FLORAL
## INSTRUCTIONS

### CHINESE DYNASTY
(SEE PAGE 21)

**FLOWERS AND GREENERY**
6 stems hypericum berries
3 stems chartreuse chrysanthemums
4 to 5 stems 'Jade' roses
6 stems ranunculus

**MATERIALS**
Chinese take-out container, plastic liner, floral knife, floral foam brick, floral clippers, floral water tubes, pair of chopsticks

**STEPS**
1. Fold in the flaps of the take-out container. Insert a plastic liner to prevent leakage.

2. With a floral knife, cut a piece of floral foam to fit snugly in the liner. Level the top of the foam so that it will not be visible. Fill the liner with room-temperature water; soak the foam in water until it is saturated.

3. Cut the stems of the hypericum berries at an angle. Insert them into the foam, making sure to position the clusters evenly.

4. Cut the stems of the chrysanthemums and roses at an angle. Gently push the stems into the foam.

5. Fill in the arrangement with ranunculus. Cut the stems at an angle. Since ranunculus are delicate and easily damaged, insert the stems into floral water tubes before arranging them.

6. For a playful look, add a pair of colorful lacquered chopsticks.

**TIPS**
Many party supply and storage stores offer take-out containers in a wide range of colors and patterns. The container should complement your decor and the theme of your party.

Use these festive take-out-container arrangements to decorate each place setting. They can also function as place cards: Label them with your guests' names and they double as lovely party favors.

**RESOURCES**
Pearl River for all things Chinese, from vases and take-out containers to fabrics, chopsticks, and paper lanterns.

The Container Store for take-out containers, string and ribbon, unusual packing materials, and gift packaging.

AsianIdeas for Chinese vases, take-out containers, chopsticks, dinnerware, parasols, and paper lanterns.

### ENGLISH ROSE
(SEE PAGE 39)

**FLOWERS AND GREENERY**
1 to 1 ½ bunches (per teacup) pink tea roses in various shades

**MATERIALS**
Porcelain teacups and saucers, floral knife, floral foam brick, floral tape, floral clippers

**STEPS**
1. Select teacups and saucers. They can be mixed and matched, vintage or new.

2. With a floral knife, cut small pieces of floral foam to fit snugly in each teacup. Level the tops of the foam pieces and secure them with floral tape. Fill the teacups with room-

temperature water; soak the foam in water until it is saturated.

3. Cut the stems of the tea roses at an angle. Working from the rim of the teacup toward the center, insert the stems into the foam in an even, compact fashion. Vary the shades to create distinction between the blooms. Make sure there are no distracting holes in your finished arrangement.

**TIPS**

Teacups and saucers are easily found at yard sales, flea markets, and secondhand stores. Look for interesting patterns and shapes.

In lieu of traditional place cards, set a teacup arrangement at each place setting. Tie handwritten labels onto the handles and they double as lovely party favors.

Don't worry if the rim of the cup has a ding; the flowers can be arranged to hide such an imperfection. However, if the arrangements will also be party favors, make sure the cups and saucers you use are in perfect condition.

Mixed-and-matched patterns are endearing, but establish a color scheme to ensure a harmonious table.

If tea roses are not available at the time of your party, any flower with a small bloom can be arranged for a similar effect.

**RESOURCES**

Authentiques Past & Present for vintage teacups and ceramics.

Woven by Water for home products and historic fabrics, including William Morris prints and English toile.

## FRENCH BOUDOIR
(SEE PAGE 61)

**FLOWERS AND GREENERY**

4 stems jasmine vines
1 bunch fresh mint (approximately 10 stems)
8 to 10 stems lavender
6 stems sweet peas
4 stems anemones
5 stems ranunculus
8 stems grape hyacinth
4 stems peonies

**MATERIALS**

Wooden box (measuring approximately 8 by 8 inches), plastic liner, floral knife, floral foam brick, floral clippers

**STEPS**

1. A wooden box, available at any container store or nursery, makes a great alternative to a traditional vase for centerpieces. Since most are not intended to hold water, insert a plastic liner to prevent leakage. If a ready-made plastic liner is unavailable, fully line the interior of the box with a piece of seamless cellophane. Trim any visible cellophane.

2. With a floral knife, cut a piece of floral foam to fit snugly in the liner. (The tighter the fit, the more surface area there will be for flowers. If the foam and liner are loose in the box, the arrangement will be unstable.) Level the top of the foam. Fill the liner with room-temperature water; soak the foam in water until it is saturated.

3. Cut the stems of the jasmine vines, mint, and lavender at an angle. Gently push the stems into the foam, making sure to position them evenly.

4. Carefully cut the fragile stems of the sweet peas, anemones, ranunculus, and grape hyacinth at an angle and gently push them into the foam. Arrange the blooms evenly into a pleasing overall shape.

5. Cut the stems of the peonies at an angle. Insert them into the foam to create focal points and to complete your arrangement.

**TIPS**

Many French boutiques carry painted wooden "fleur" boxes with stenciled words on them. If you are unable to find these, you can easily create your own: Hand-paint any wooden box with craft paint; when the paint is dry, stencil words onto one side.

To create an aged look or distressed surface, lightly sand the box with fine sandpaper.

For a French country "just-picked" look, arrange the flowers loosely.

**RESOURCES**

McCann Brothers for wooden "fleur" boxes and other French country-inspired containers, such as tins and baskets.

## INDIAN SARI
(SEE PAGE 68)

**FLOWERS AND GREENERY**
10 stems citronella
5 stems calla lilies
7 to 10 stems marigolds
8 stems 'Léonidas' roses
5 stems lotus pods
7 stems rose hip berries

**MATERIALS**
Glass cylindrical vase (approximately 6 inches tall and 7 inches in diameter), clear carpet or double-stick tape, silk ribbon (determine the yardage based on the size of the selected vase), fabric scissors, floral knife, floral foam brick, floral clippers

**STEPS**
1. Wrap a cylindrical vase completely with carpet tape.

2. Adhere ribbon to the sticky surface of the carpet tape. Begin at the bottom of the vase and wrap the ribbon around and around, making sure to slightly overlap the edges. At the top, neatly cut the ribbon with fabric scissors. Fold the end in to hide the raw edge and to keep it from unraveling. Secure the folded end with a small piece of carpet tape.

3. With a floral knife, cut a piece of floral foam to fit snugly in the vase. Level the top of the foam so that it will not be visible. Fill the vase with room-temperature water; soak the foam in water until it is saturated.

4. Cut the stems of the citronella at an angle. Insert them into the foam.

5. Cut the stems of the calla lilies, marigolds, and 'Léonidas' roses at an angle. Gently push the stems into the foam. Start with the calla lilies since their stems are more fragile and have a tendency to bend. Add the marigolds, and then the 'Léonidas' roses.

6. Fill in with lotus pods and rose hip berries. Cut the stems at an angle and gently push them into the foam to complete your festive Indian-inspired arrangement.

**TIPS**
Select a solid-colored ribbon as a vase covering. Printed and embroidered ribbons may be substituted provided that they do not compete with the flowers.

For an Indian-inspired arrangement, select a colorful mix of jewel-toned flowers. Drape a sari or a piece of sumptuous silk around the base of your vase.

**RESOURCES**
Mokuba New York for silk ribbon.

Royal Sari House for Indian textiles, such as saris and silks.

## JAPANESE KIMONO
(SEE PAGE 88)

**FLOWERS AND GREENERY**
8 to 10 stems lemon leaves
5 stems calla lilies
1 dozen white roses
6 stems peonies
6 to 8 stems scabiosa

**MATERIALS**
Glass cylinder vase, scissors, printed papers, medium-size flat paintbrush, Mod Podge, double-faced satin ribbon, fabric or craft glue, floral knife, floral foam brick, floral tape, floral clippers

**STEPS**
1. Cut strips of assorted printed and solid handmade papers to the height of the vase. Vary the width of the strips to create interest.

2. Once the strips are cut, you are ready to decorate the vase. With a paintbrush, cover the entire vase with a thin coat of Mod Podge. Place the strips of paper onto the sticky surface in a vertical direction. Make sure to slightly overlap the edges of each strip to ensure full coverage.

3. Once the vase is completely covered in paper and the adhesive is dry, you are ready to add the ribbon. Cut strips of ribbon to the

height of the vase. Using fabric or craft glue, conceal the seams of the paper with the ribbon. Neatly trim any excess. Once the adhesive is dry, glue ribbons horizontally around the top and bottom of the vase. You can also create an obilike "sash" for the vase by gluing a wider ribbon around the center. Finish by tying a narrower ribbon over the sash with a simple knot.

4. With a floral knife, cut a piece of floral foam to fit snugly in the vase. Level the top of the foam so that it will not be visible. Fill the vase with room-temperature water; soak the foam in water until it is saturated. Secure the foam with floral tape placed in an "x" formation.

5. Cut the stems of the lemon leaves at an angle. Insert them into the foam, fully covering it and the floral tape. This greenery will provide a lovely backdrop for your blooms.

6. Cut the stems of the flowers at an angle. Insert them into the foam tightly. Begin with the calla lilies; add the white roses, peonies, and scabiosa. Your finished arrangement should be round and compact.

### TIPS
When creating an arrangement for a dining room table, make sure to keep the flowers low. There is nothing worse than a game of peekaboo around a centerpiece.

### RESOURCES
A. I. Friedman for handmade papers, ribbon, and art supplies.

Jamali Garden Supplies for glass and ceramic vases, pots, and floral supplies.

Kate's Paperie for handmade and unusual printed papers.

Paper Access for unusual printed papers.

## MEXICAN ALTAR
(SEE PAGE 106)

### FLOWERS AND GREENERY
25 to 30 carnations in various shades of the same color

### MATERIALS
Distressed or vintage tin or sap bucket (measuring approximately 8 inches high by 8 inches in diameter), plastic liner, floral knife, floral foam brick, floral tape, floral clippers

### STEPS
1. Since vintage tins and sap buckets are often not watertight, insert a plastic liner into your vessel to prevent leakage. If a ready-made plastic liner is not available, fully line the interior of the vessel with a piece of seamless cellophane. Trim any visible cellophane.

2. With a floral knife, cut a piece of floral foam to fit snugly in the liner. Level the top of the foam. Fill the liner with room-temperature water; soak the foam in water until it is saturated. Secure the foam with floral tape placed in an "x" formation.

3. Cut the stems of the carnations at an angle. Insert the stems into the foam in an even, compact fashion, making sure to fill any holes in your composition. Vary the shades of the blooms to create distinction between them.

### TIPS
Keeping the arrangement tight and compact gives carnations—once considered a passé flower—a modern and ruffly look. Carnations mixed with other flowers feel dated and are a big no-no in my book.

Monochromatic flowers, as well as those in different shades of the same color, look sophisticated and have a strong impact.

Carnations are a hearty flower, perfect for finicky climates and for arrangements that need to last for weeks.

Glue felt tabs to the bottoms of rustic containers to protect your tables from scratches and moisture.

### RESOURCES
Great Stuff by Paul Antiques for sap buckets, furniture, and unusual old finds.

La Sirena for all things Mexican, from folk and religious art, *botanica* candles, and charms to paper goods, vinyl oilcloths, and fiesta party supplies.

## MOROCCAN MEDINA
(SEE PAGE 124)

### FLOWERS AND GREENERY
4 stems lemon branches with fruit attached
10 stems 'Red Robin' photinia
8 to 10 stems vanda orchids
1 dozen 'Gold Strike' roses

### MATERIALS
Terra-cotta pot, plastic liner, floral knife, floral foam brick, floral clippers, floral water tubes

### STEPS
1. Line a terra-cotta pot (one that is aged, if possible) with a plastic liner to prevent leakage. If a ready-made plastic liner is unavailable, fully line the interior of the pot with a piece of seamless cellophane. Trim any visible cellophane.

2. With a floral knife, cut a piece of floral foam to fit snugly in the liner. Fill the liner with room-temperature water; soak the foam in water until it is saturated.

3. Cut the lemon branches at an angle. Insert them into the foam. Allow the fruit to hang over the edge of the pot to soften the arrangement.

4. After the lemon branches are positioned, cut the stems of 'Red Robin' photinia at an angle. Insert them into the foam to create interest and to frame the orchids.

5. Add the vanda orchids. Cut the stems at an angle. If the stems are too short for your composition, insert them into floral water tubes to add height. Gently push the tubes into the foam.

6. Cut the stems of the 'Gold Strike' roses at an angle and insert them into the foam to complete your arrangement.

### TIPS
If lemon branches with fruit are unavailable, purchase individual lemons, pierce each one with a wooden skewer, then cluster and insert them into your arrangement to create a natural effect.

For added color and drama, scatter loose lemons on the table around your arrangement, or pile them in a bowl placed nearby.

Other fruits and vegetables, such as artichokes, grapes, pomegranates, figs, and oranges, are also perfect for arrangements. Match the fruits or vegetables you use to the season and occasion.

For a Moroccan-inspired event, lay woven Berber runners on your table or buffet.

### RESOURCES
Imports from Marrakech Ltd., Chelsea Market, for all things Moroccan, from pillows, rugs, *tagines*, and ceramics to lanterns, tiles, furniture, and glassware.

Jamali Garden Supplies for terra-cotta pots, floral supplies, ribbon, and glassware.

## SOUTHERN ROOTS
(SEE PAGE 155)

### FLOWERS AND GREENERY
5 to 6 stems hydrangeas
12 stems scabiosa
8 stems lisianthus

### MATERIALS
Ceramic water pitcher, floral knife, floral foam brick, hammer, floral clippers

### STEPS
1. With a floral knife, cut a piece of floral foam to fit snugly in the ceramic pitcher. Level the top of the foam. Fill the pitcher with room-temperature water; soak the foam in water until it is saturated.

2. Cut the stems of hydrangeas at an angle and smash the ends with a hammer. Insert them into the foam.

3. Cut the stems of scabiosa and lisianthus at an angle. Gently push the stems into the foam to complete your arrangement.

### TIPS
Hydrangea is a hearty bloom but sensitive to the environment. If the florets are not firm to the touch, or if they are beginning to wilt, set a wet paper towel over them and leave

until it is dry. (Hydrangea drinks through the bloom as well as the stem.)

When using multiple blooms, keep the palette monochromatic for a more modern and sophisticated look.

Rustic antique ceramic jugs or plain pottery water pitchers are a great alternative to traditional vases.

### RESOURCES
Appley Hoare Antiques for fine European antique furniture and accessories.

## TROPICAL RAIN FOREST
(SEE PAGE 172)

### FLOWERS AND GREENERY
6 stems lady's mantles
4 stems hypericum berries
2 stems protea
4 stems 'Léonidas' roses
3 stems 'Jade' roses
4 stems ranunculus
2 stems mango calla lilies
6 stems Billy's buttons

### MATERIALS
Coffee tin, plastic liner, floral knife, floral foam brick, floral tape, floral clippers, floral water tubes

### STEPS
1. Use a colorful coffee tin found in any grocery store as a vase. Empty the contents and thoroughly wash the tin. If it is not watertight, line it with a plastic liner. If a ready-made plastic liner is unavailable, fully line the interior with a piece of seamless cellophane. Trim any visible cellophane.

2. With a floral knife, cut a piece of floral foam to fit snugly in the tin (or liner). Level the top of the foam. Fill the tin (or liner) with room-temperature water; soak the foam in water until it is saturated. Secure the foam with floral tape placed in an "x" formation.

3. Cut the stems of the lady's mantles and hypericum berries at an angle. Insert the stems into the foam at the desired height; making sure to compose the greenery so it covers the foam.

4. Add the largest flower heads—the protea and the roses. Cut the stems at an angle and insert them into the foam.

5. Fill in the arrangement with the smaller headed-flowers—the ranunculus, calla lilies, and Billy's buttons—to add contrasting textures and colors. Cut the ranunculus and calla lily stems at an angle and insert them into water tubes. Cut the Billy's buttons at an angle. Gently push the ranunculus, calla lilies, and BIlly's buttons into the foam to complete your arrangement.

### TIPS
Some flowers have delicate stems and will snap if not properly placed. Floral water tubes will help to protect the stems and ensure easier manipulation.

Use printed tins in various sizes to create whimsical compositions. Lining several of them down the center of a table is a great alternative to a traditional centerpiece.

Use large, tropical leaves on the table in place of fabric runners and placemats. They will serve the same purpose but are unusually clever. If tropical leaves are not native to your environment, or unavailable through your local florist, there are realistic silk alternatives on the market that will fool even the most knowledgeable guests.

### RESOURCES
Caribbean Cuts for tropical flowers and leaves.

Pany Silk Flowers Corporation for silk flowers and leaves.

# FAVORITE HAUNTS

## FOR FLORAL DISPLAY

FOR *FLOWERS FOR THE HOME* I have used a variety of blooms and foliage to create floral arrangements inspired by places near and far. Many are available at your local florist shop. Most of the following select resources offer online services. Sources are also provided for each of the nine locales featured in this book.

**GENERAL SUPPLIES AND CONTAINERS**

**AFLORAL.COM**
www.afloral.com
Floral supplies

**B & J FLORIST SUPPLY CO.**
103 West 28th Street
New York, New York 10001
(212) 564-6086
Glass and ceramic vases, pots, floral supplies

**THE HOME DEPOT**
www.homedepot.com
Garden supplies, tools

**JAMALI GARDEN SUPPLIES**
149 West 28th Street
New York, New York 10001
(212) 244-4025
www.jamaligarden.com
Glass and ceramic vases, pots, floral supplies

**LOWE'S**
www.lowes.com
Lawn and garden supplies, planters, pots

**MICHAELS**
www.michaels.com
Art and craft supplies

**SMITH & HAWKEN**
www.smithandhawken.com
Garden supplies, outdoor furniture

**ART SUPPLIES**

**A. I. FRIEDMAN**
44 West 18th Street
New York, New York 10011
(212) 243-9000
www.aifriedman.com
Printed papers, art supplies

**THE CONTAINER STORE**
www.containerstore.com
Take-out containers, tins, ribbon, string, gift packaging

**KATE'S PAPERIE**
www.katespaperie.com
Handmade and printed papers, ribbon, gift packaging

**PAPER ACCESS**
23 West 18th Street
New York, New York 10011
(800) 727-3701
www.paperpresentation.com
Printed papers, art supplies

**HOME FURNISHINGS AND ACCESSORIES**

**ABC CARPET AND HOME**
888 Broadway
New York, New York 10003
(212) 473-3000
www.abchome.com
Home furnishings, antiques, lighting, tableware, bedding, "green" products, ethnic objects

**APPLEY HOARE ANTIQUES**
22 Pimlico Road
London SW1W 8LJ
England
020 7730 7070
www.appleyhoare.com
Fine European antique furniture and home furnishings

**CLODAGH**
670 Broadway, 4th floor
New York, New York 10012
(212) 780-5300
www.clodagh.com
Modern, ethnic furniture and accessories, feng shui-inspired design services

**ELLEN CHRISTINE MILLINERY**
255 West 18th Street
New York, New York 10011
(212) 242-2457
www.ellenchristine.com
Period and custom-made hats and accessories, vintage textiles

**FELIX POPULI**
V.R.S.U.P., Inc.
PO Box 1323
New York, New York 10113
(646) 454-9394
www.felixpopuli.com
Tabletop items, pillows, linens, wall decor

**GREAT STUFF BY PAUL ANTIQUES**
257 6th at East Street
Frederick, Maryland 21701
(301) 631-5340
www.greatstuffbypaul.com
Vintage finds, sap buckets, furniture

**HOMART**
15041-A Bake Parkway
Irvine, California 92618
(888) 346-6278
www.homart.com
Home accessories, gifts

**TAKASHIMAYA NEW YORK**
693 Fifth Avenue
New York, New York 10022
(212) 350-0100
www.takashimaya-ny.com
Japanese home furnishings, including lacquerware, trays, ceramic and stoneware bowls and vases, tea

**RESOURCES FOR *FLOWERS FOR THE HOME* ARRANGEMENTS AND TABLETOPS**

**CHINESE DYNASTY**

**ASIANIDEAS**
www.asianideas.com
Tea services, paper lanterns, parasols, silk fabrics, furniture

**THE CONTAINER STORE**
Take-out containers, tins, ribbon, string, gift packaging
(See Art Supplies listing.)

**PEARL RIVER**
477 Broadway
New York, New York 10013
(212) 431-4770
www.pearlriver.com
Dinnerware, tea services, paper lanterns, parasols, fans, silk fabrics, clothing, carved deities, furniture, waving kitties, incense and holders

**ENGLISH ROSE**

**AUTHENTIQUES PAST & PRESENT**
255 West 18th Street
New York, New York 10011
(212) 675-2179
Vintage teacups and saucers, vases, Christmas ornaments

**ELLEN CHRISTINE MILLINERY**
Period and custom-made hats, accessories, vintage textiles
(See Home Furnishings and Accessories listing.)

**HOMART**
Home accessories, gifts, crown-shaped vases
(See Home Furnishings and Accessories listing.)

**WEDGWOOD**
www.wedgwoodusa.com
Fine bone china, dinnerware, home accessories

**WOVEN BY WATER**
PO Box 235
Sedona, Arizona 86339
(928) 282-6490
www.wovenbywater.com
Historical fabrics, including William Morris prints

**FRENCH BOUDOIR**

**ELLEN CHRISTINE MILLINERY**
Period and custom-made hats, accessories, vintage textiles
(See Home Furnishings and Accessories listing.)

**McCANN BROTHERS BASKETS**
261 River Street
Bridgeport, Connecticut 06604
(203) 335-8630
www.mccannbaskets.com
Baskets, tins, pots, wooden "fleur" boxes

**INDIAN SARI**

**MOKUBA NEW YORK**
55 West 39th Street
New York, New York 10018
(212) 869-8900
www.mokubany.com
Fine ribbon

**ROYAL SARI HOUSE**
264 Fifth Avenue
New York, New York 10001
(212) 679-0732
Traditional Indian clothing and accessories, including saris

**JAPANESE KIMONO**

**A. I. FRIEDMAN**
Printed papers, art supplies
(See Art Supplies listing.)

**JAMALI GARDEN SUPPLIES**
Glass and ceramic vases, pots, floral supplies
(See General Supplies and Containers listing.)

**KATE'S PAPERIE**
Hand-made and printed papers, ribbon, gift packaging
(See Art Supplies listing.)

**MIYA SHOJI**
109 West 17th Street
New York, New York 10011
(212) 243-6774
www.miyashoji.com
Shoji screens, custom furniture

**PAPER ACCESS**
Printed papers, art supplies
(See Art Supplies listing.)

**TAKASHIMAYA NEW YORK**
Lacquerware, tea
(See Home Furnishings and Accessories listing.)

**MEXICAN ALTAR**

**GREAT STUFF BY PAUL ANTIQUES**
Vintage finds, sap buckets, furniture
(See Home Furnishings and Accessories listing.)

**LA SIRENA**
27 East 3rd Street
New York, New York 10003
(212) 780-9113
www.lasirenanyc.com
Mexican folk and religious art, paper goods, *botanica* candles, fiesta party supplies

**MOROCCAN MEDINA**

**FELIX POPULI**
Tabletop items, pillows, linens, wall decor
(See Home Furnishings and Accessories listing.)

**IMPORTS OF MARRAKECH LTD.**
**CHELSEA MARKET**
88 Tenth Avenue
New York, New York 10011
(212) 675-9700
www.importsfrommarrakesh.com
Moroccan lanterns, pillows, rugs, tiles, *tagines*, glassware, ceramics, furniture

**JAMALI GARDEN SUPPLIES**
Glass and ceramic vases, pots, floral supplies
(See General Supplies and Containers listing.)

**SOUTHERN ROOTS**

**ELLEN CHRISTINE MILLINERY**
Period and custom-made hats and accessories, including doll-head vases
(See Home Furnishings and Accessories listing.)

**FELIX POPULI**
Tabletop items, pillows, linens, wall decor
(See Home Furnishings and Accessories listing.)

**GREAT STUFF BY PAUL ANTIQUES**
Vintage finds, sap buckets, furniture
(See Home Furnishings and Accessories listing.)

**TROPICAL RAIN FOREST**

**CARIBBEAN CUTS**
120 West 28th Street
New York, New York 10001
(212) 924-6969
www.caribbeancuts.com
Tropical flowers, leaves, vessels

**CLODAGH**
Modern, ethnic furniture and accessories, including grass matting and hammered metal basins, feng shui-inspired design services
(See Home Furnishings and Accessories listing.)

**PANY SILK FLOWERS CORPORATION**
146 West 28th Street
New York, New York 10001
(212) 645-9526
Fine silk flowers and leaves

# Acknowledgments

I WOULD LIKE to thank the following individuals for all their help and support during the production of *Flowers for the Home*. First, to Arturo Quintero, my rock and co-owner of Prudence Designs, who introduced me to the art of flower arranging.

To the team behind the book, who worked so tirelessly to publish my vision. To publisher Charles Miers, special projects editor Sandy Gilbert, and everyone else at Rizzoli International Publications who believed in the book from the beginning. Sandy not only held my hand throughout my first book but she also enthusiastically helped with the propping and styling of the photography and text research. To Ellen Silverman for shooting such breathtaking photographs, and Kevin Norris who assisted and made the process so enjoyable. To Ivette Montes de Oca, who brought her artistic vision to the book's design and photography. To the following individuals who finessed the text: Susan Homer, Hilary Ney, and Elizabeth Smith. To Paulette Cole for her generous foreword. And to Tracey Zabar, who helped me find my words and added her own voice, as well as for her extensive research.

To the Prudence Designs team, whose great talents made this book a reality—office manager Thomas O'Laughlin, who organizes my life, florists Marlene Fusaris and Amy Greenough, and Rogellio Balbuena, Johnny Diaz, and Tina Wrightman. To Cathy King for her colorful pottery that wonderfully complements our arrangements.

To Kim Ronemus (my forever twin), Anita Trehan (my Indian princess), and to the rest of my family of friends who have been both coaches and cheerleaders in my life: Laurie Joachim, Gia Grosso, Yasmine St. James, Todd Soyars, John Rosado, Dan Williams, and Philippe Mayor. To Tricia Foley and Karan Trehan, who allowed me to use their beautiful homes, full of such inspiring furnishings, as locations for some of the photography. And thank you to all who generously lent such glorious objects and textiles for the book's photography. A special thanks goes to Margo Montaquila, Michelle Westcott-Richards, Dina Leor, Ben Sander, Wilkie Wong, Tom Tran, Ellen Christine, Mohamed Elmaarouf, Kate Hirson, Amy Nebens, James Cook Embree Jr., and Maria McBride. And to the Zabars—David, Benjamin, Marki, Daniel, Michael, William, and Mary Rose.

To my Venezuelan family whose support over the many years has meant the world to me—Teresa, Lucho, Minerva, Milagros, Fernando, and Maria Fernanda. And to Miriam and Gabriel, who feel like family. And finally, to my family—my late father who encouraged my creativity and to my mother for her insight, advice, and friendship. To my sister, Kelly, and to Jerry, Jordan, and McKenna.

May the
beauty
of flowers
always
illuminate
your travels.